THE M1
CARBINE

ROGER OUT

THE M1 CARBINE

CLASSIC **GUNS** OF THE **WORLD** SERIES

M1 CARBINE

MARKINGS

VARIANTS

AMMUNITION

ACCESSORIES

SCHIFFER MILITARY
4880 Lower Valley Road   Atglen, PA 19310

Library of Congress Control Number: 2020943655

Cover design by Justin Watkinson
Type set in Helvetica Neue LT Pro/Times New Roman

ISBN: 978-0-7643-6189-0
Printed in India

Published by Schiffer Publishing, Ltd.
4880 Lower Valley Road
Atglen, PA 19310
Phone: (610) 593-1777; Fax: (610) 593-2002
E-mail: Info@schifferbooks.com
Web: www.schifferbooks.com

For our complete selection of fine books on this and related subjects,
please visit our website at www.schifferbooks.com.
You may also write for a free catalog.

Schiffer Publishing's titles are available at special discounts for
bulk purchases for sales promotions or premiums. Special editions,
including personalized covers, corporate imprints, and excerpts,
can be created in large quantities for special needs.
For more information, contact the publisher.

We are always looking for people to write books on new
and related subjects. If you have an idea for a book,
please contact us at proposals@schifferbooks.com.

CONTENTS

CHAPTER 1

ORIGINS AND DEVELOPMENT

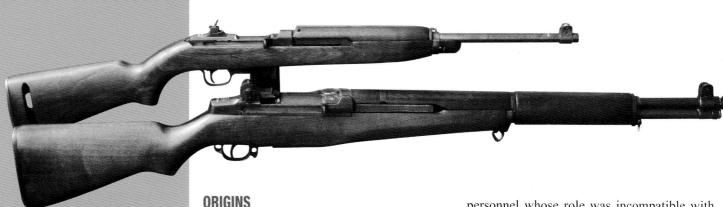

The carbine and the M1 Garand rifle. The rifle ammunition offers a power and range far superior to that of the carbine, but its size and weight make it too bulky for use by soldiers assigned to specialist tasks (those using heavy weapons, drivers, radio operators, et al.).

ORIGINS

When the United States entered the war in 1917, the majority of American infantrymen were equipped with Springfield 1903 and US 17 rifles.[1]

These shoulder arms, although excellent for the basic foot soldier, proved to be far too bulky for any kind of technical use even though these technical uses were becoming increasingly more important throughout the conflict.[2]

There was insufficient time to develop an interim weapon specifically destined for these combatants whose principal mission did not require the use of an individual weapon. They were, however, generally equipped with a handgun,[3] the best solution at that time. For a long time, the majority of soldiers had been aware of the weak offensive value of the handguns, and this notion was confirmed by statistical studies carried out after the war, which showed that only a very small proportion of wounds inflicted on enemy fighters originated from handguns.

A great number of reports recommended the development of a light automatic carbine to arm personnel whose role was incompatible with carrying an infantry rifle. However, the budgetary restrictions imposed by the economic context of the twenties did not allow the development of such a weapon to be undertaken. The rare credits available to study new individual weapons went, as a priority, to development programs focusing on the semiautomatic rifle which culminated in 1936 with the adoption of the M1 Garand.

In addition, it was apparent that neither the model 1906 .30-caliber cartridge used by shoulder arms, light machine guns, and machine guns nor the .45 cartridge used with handguns and the Thompson submachine gun was suitable for the planned light carbine. The first cartridge was too powerful, and the second presented mediocre ballistic features. The adoption of a light carbine therefore entailed the adoption of a new type of ammunition with all the associated logistical problems. A great number of senior military personnel were totally opposed to the adoption of an interim weapon using a new type of ammunition.

1. The Model 1897 Winchester pump-action shotgun was also used by the US Army. However, since the use of nonjacketed bullets was contrary to The Hague Convention, this raised vehement protests from the German authorities. In order to avoid these facts from being exploited by the enemy for propaganda purposes, as well as reprisals against combatants captured in possession of a pump-action shotgun, the American commander chose swiftly to limit the use of these "trench guns" to the guarding of premises and prisoners behind front lines.
2. Such as artillerymen, drivers, users of machine guns, radio operators, or liaison agents, for example.
3. Principally, Colt M1911 semiautomatic pistols, and Colt and Smith & Wesson model 1917 revolvers.

Soldiers from the American Expeditionary Force, photographed in France during the First World War. The man in the foreground is armed with a Springfield 1903 rifle.
l'Illustration

Winchester semiautomatic carbine 351 SL caliber, with a Colt 1911 and various accessories evoking French aviation of the First World War. The carbine pictured here is equipped with a twenty-round magazine of the type used in France to arm the crews of the first airplanes. There is no doubt that the Winchester carbine influenced the development of the M1 carbine. *Marc de Fromont*

In 1938, the commander of the infantry issued a new request to research a light carbine to arm men with technical tasks and ammunition suppliers. No further action was taken on this until the outbreak of the Second World War, which brought into focus the need for a compact individual weapon, firing intermediate-power ammunition between that of a rifle and a pistol.

Unlike the previous conflict where French operations took place mostly on a relatively static front, this new conflict was a war of movement where motorized columns and groups of parachutists and motorcyclists could penetrate far behind enemy lines and carry out surprise attacks on headquarters or units that would not have been threatened at all during the previous conflict.

In June 1940, a new request from the general staff of the infantry was considered by the War Department, which gave the order to the US Army Ordnance Department to develop a weapon weighing less than 5 pounds, and able to be carried on a sling and with effective fire up to 300 yards.

DEVELOPMENT

Since neither the semiautomatic carbines nor the cartridges commercially available corresponded exactly to what was needed, a team from the Ordnance Department, placed under the direction of Maj. René Studler, drew up the specifications for the new weapon and its ammunition.

For the development of the latter, a direct appeal was made to the Winchester-Western firm, which, after a rapid study, proposed a .30-caliber (7.62 mm) cartridge, derived from ammunition formerly developed for the model 1905

Three types of weapons commonly used for personal protection: the Thompson 1928 A1 machine pistol, the M1 carbine, and the Colt 1911. The carbine represents an excellent compromise between the heavy and bulky machine pistol and the pistol with its insufficient range and mediocre accuracy beyond a few dozen meters.

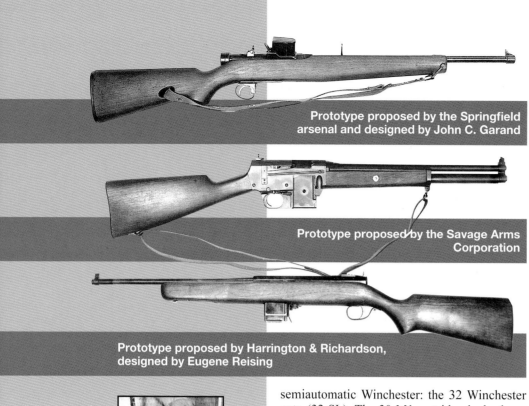

Prototype proposed by the Springfield arsenal and designed by John C. Garand

Prototype proposed by the Savage Arms Corporation

Prototype proposed by Harrington & Richardson, designed by Eugene Reising

Edwin Pugsley, head of production at Winchester, showing one of the first M1 made by his company. *Cody Firearms Museum*

Jonathan Edmund Browning

semiautomatic Winchester: the 32 Winchester auto (32 SL). The 30 M1 cartridge had a huge advantage over the majority of military ammunition of the period since it had a noncorrosive primer.[4] From June 1941 on, nine prototypes designed by different inventors and based on the specifications established by the Ordnance Department were submitted for military tests:

• two proposed by the Springfield arsenal (one of which had been designed by John C. Garand, creator of the regulation semiautomatic rifle adopted by the US Army, four years previously)

• one by Savage Arm Corporation

• one designed by Eugene Reising, presented by the Harrington & Richardson company

• one prototype proposed by Colt

• one model proposed by the Auto-Ordnance firm (which had developed the Thompson machine pistol)

• one model presented by the Woodhull Corporation

• a weapon conceived by George Hyde and made by Bendix Aviation Corporation

• a weapon in system White .276 caliber, which was immediately eliminated since it was not designed for the ammunition type chosen by the army

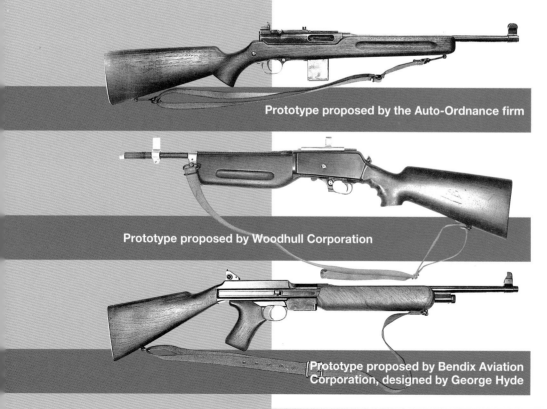

Prototype proposed by the Auto-Ordnance firm

Prototype proposed by Woodhull Corporation

Prototype proposed by Bendix Aviation Corporation, designed by George Hyde

4. The .30-06 used by Springfield rifles, US 17, and M1 Garand, however. did have a corrosive primer. Bearing in mind the difficulties of maintaining weapons in operation, it is understandable that the majority of Garand rifles found on the terrain have very oxidized barrels, whereas those of M1 carbines with the same provenance were often in perfect condition.

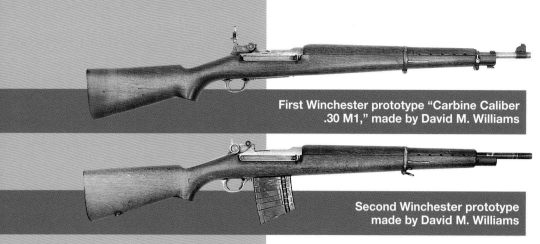

First Winchester prototype "Carbine Caliber .30 M1," made by David M. Williams

Second Winchester prototype made by David M. Williams

American paratrooper photographed during training. For this type of situation, the light and easy-to-handle M1 was much more comfortable to carry than the Garand.
US Signal Corps

Only the carbines created by John Garand (Springfield Arsenal) and George Hyde (Bendix Aviation Corporation) were retained after the initial tests in anticipation of a new campaign of testing programmed for September 1941.

From before the war, the Winchester firm was interested in developing a light semiautomatic weapon using a mechanism conceived by Jonathan Edmund Browning, half brother of the famous weapon designer John Moses Browning. Despite the firm already being committed to the production of the Garand rifle, it did not present any prototype to the test of June 1941.

After the sudden death of Jonathan Edmund Browning in May 1939, following a bout of appendicitis, Winchester entrusted the development of the project to David Marshall Williams. This colorful character, having served prison time for bootlegging during Prohibition, dedicated himself to the work of a gunsmith, for which he showed real aptitude. He was responsible for more than forty patents on weapon mechanisms, among them developments on the floating chamber system used by the .22-caliber training version of the Browning 1917 and 1919 model machine gun and the Colt 1911 A1 pistol (Ace Service Model).

Williams resolved the initial operation problems of J. E. Browning's weapon by applying a system of his own conception: the short-stroke gas piston.

Thanks to this principle, which will be examined later, Winchester was able to present a carbine that outclassed the other models in the running in the military tests of September 1941, and it was adopted by the United States Army in the last days of October 1941 under the name "Carbine, Caliber .30 M1." The manufacture of these M1 carbines started in June 1941 at Inland, a division of the General Motors Corporation. The first weapons were delivered to the army for inspection in August 1942. At Winchester, production started in September.

Subsequently, eight other firms produced M1 carbines, calling on dozens of other establishments as subcontractors for various constituent parts. We will return to the different manufacturers and to the modifications that were made during the manufacture of the initial model later in this edition.

It had initially been planned to make 500,000 carbines. The success of the weapon was such that demand grew constantly throughout the war, and the total number of carbines produced at the end of the conflict reached more than six million.

US transmission post during the Second World War; noncombatant troops were equipped with the USM1 carbine.
US Army

DAVID MARSHALL WILLIAMS
AN EXTRAORDINARY MAN

David Marshall Williams was born in 1900 on a farm in Godwin, North Carolina. At the end of his teenage years, Williams tried to sign up to the Navy, but the war in Europe had just finished and the Navy had become more attentive on the issue of recruitment and refused his request. The era of Prohibition in the United States gave young adventurous people, with scant respect for the law, an opportunity to earn quick money. Williams set up a secret distillery near the parental farm and was later arrested because of an incident during which a deputy sheriff was killed.

In 1919, the nineteen-year-old Williams was sentenced to thirty years' imprisonment. Doubts remained concerning his direct involvement in a murder, which prevented him from receiving the death penalty.

After several years of incarceration, Williams was transferred to a closed prison, where he gained permission to use the metal workshop and began making models of mechanisms that he had imagined during his years of incarceration. Impressed by the ideas of this model prisoner, the prison authorities authorized him to pursue his research, which resulted in various patents, including one for the floating chamber and the captive piston.

After having his sentence reduced, Williams returned to the family farm in Godwin, where he set up his own gunsmith workshop.

The patent of his floating-chamber mechanism was bought by Colt, which adapted it to its .22R-caliber version of the 1911

David Marshall Williams, inventor of the captive piston principle and many other weapon mechanisms: one of the fathers of the M1 rifle

Colt: the Ace Service model and a reduced-fire version of the Browning machine gun.

Several years later, Winchester called on Williams to conclude the development of the weapon left unfinished due to the death of Jonathan Edmund Browning. Williams resolved the main operational problems by applying himself to the task, which later became the M1 carbine, its captive piston patent, and various improvements. Incontestably, the former prisoner had a major part in the birth of the famous M1 American carbine.

On the other hand, it would appear that this highly individualistic character had difficulty in integrating the research team at Winchester and that he scarcely had more than a passive, and sometimes even disruptive, role in the final developments of the weapon.

In 1952, the director Richard Thorpe brought a biography of Williams to the screen in which the title role was played by James Stewart. The film, *Carbine Williams*, depicts a highly romanticized version of his life.

Promoted to the rank of patriotic hero, David Williams died in 1975. Four years earlier he had donated the entire contents of his workshop—machines, tools, and prototypes of weapons—to the North Carolina Museum of History. After several years of exhibition in its own premises, the North Carolina Museum of History re-created Williams's workshop at a site in the town of Raleigh, where it can be visited today.

"Thirteen Day" Winchester prototype by David M. Williams, made in thirteen days

View of the machines producing the carbine barrels in the Winchester factory during the war

This German soldier has given up his service weapon in favor of an M1 carbine captured from the American army during the Battle of the Bulge. *Bundesarchiv*

PRESENTATION

GENERAL POINTS

As is often the case with successful weapons, the operation of the M1 carbine uses extremely simple principles, and its mechanism has few parts.

It is a semiautomatic shoulder weapon, with fixed bolt, operated by indirect action of gases on the actuator by means of a captive piston. The weapon is fed by a removable magazine with eight rounds in a double-stack, double-feed arrangement, which presents alternatively on each lip of the magazine.

Series versions have a fifteen-round magazine. A thirty-round magazine would be adopted in 1945.

The weapon has a safety with a catch (which was to be replaced by a lever) placed at the front of the trigger guard, behind the magazine bolt lever.

Subsequently, several other weapons derived from the M1 carbine were developed:

- the M1A1 carbine, fitted with a fold-back buttstock and destined for use by airborne troops

- the M2 carbine, fitted with a fire mode selector allowing for the choice of single-shot or continuous-burst fire

- the M3 carbine, adapted for the use of a sight coupled with a projector of infrared rays

These three variations are presented in chapter 6.

OPERATION

The locking of the bolt is carried out by two lugs positioned at the front of the bolt in a diametrically opposite position. These lugs are in housings machined in the receiver. The one on the right is extended by a cam that slides in a groove situated on the internal side of the bolt handle, which extends the slide. The unlocking and locking rails are carried in this groove.

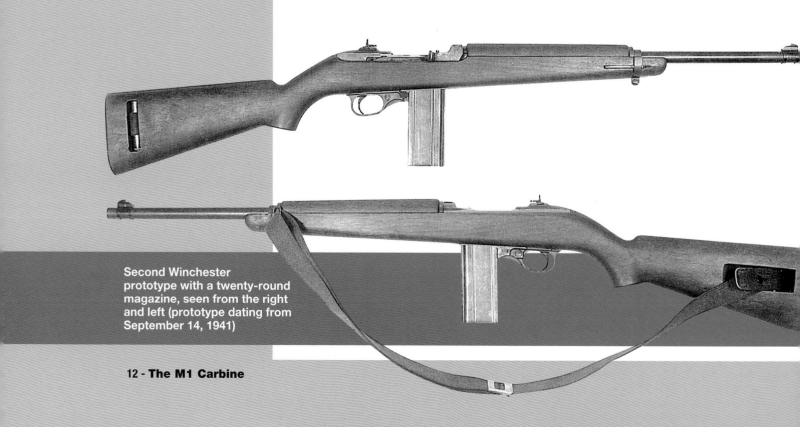

Second Winchester prototype with a twenty-round magazine, seen from the right and left (prototype dating from September 14, 1941)

The moment a shot is fired, the projectile goes past a gas port pierced in the lower part of the barrel around 13.5 cm in front of the chamber, and a portion of the gas produced by the combustion of the propulsive charge rushes into a chamber via the gas port adjacent to the barrel, containing a captive piston with a limited route (3.5 mm).

The impulse imparted to the piston by the gas is of such an intensity that the short recoil of the piston is sufficient to push the actuator to the rear.

Guided forward by flanges and to the rear by the operating-slide guideway lug, the slide moves back only around 8 mm, then the unlocking rail raises the cam extending the right lug, making the bolt turn on its axis. This causes unlocking in the true sense. The bolt can then accompany the slide in its rearward movement. The extractor positioned on the right side of the head of the bolt pulls the empty shell from the chamber.

As soon as the shell has totally left the chamber, the ejector, in constant contact with its spring, throws it upward and to the right.

During the rearward movement, the hammer, pushed by the bolt, hooks on to the trigger bar.

When the mobile parts are stopped, the recoil spring, compressed in its housing, relaxes and sends the parts forward. The bolt strips a cartridge from the clip during this movement and guides it into the chamber.

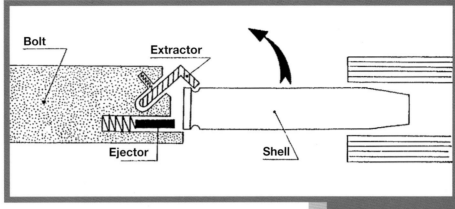

At the end of the forward movement, the locking rail lowers the right lug, the bolt pivots, and its lugs return to their position in their housing. After a rotation of about 30 degrees to the right, locking takes place, and it is caught by the cartridge groove extractor. The trigger, until now positioned at half cock, goes to full cock; the weapon is now ready to fire again.

In order to prevent any firing of a cartridge before the closure of the bolt, the mechanism was designed so that the hammer cannot hit the base of the firing pin and the firing pin cannot project into the striker hole before locking is complete.

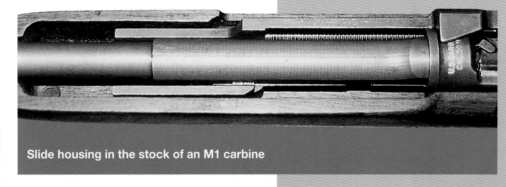

Slide housing in the stock of an M1 carbine

FEATURES

Caliber	7.62 mm (.30-caliber carbine ammunition)
Total length	90 cm
Barrel length	46 cm (four grooves, right-handed rifling, 50.8 cm or 20 inches)
Line-of-sight length	56 cm
Weight	2.35 kg
Grooves	four grooves, 50.8 cm
Magazine capacity	

Fifteen or thirty cartridges (magazines of five cartridges were also made after the war for the carbine to be used as a hunting or sport weapon in countries not permitting the use of large-capacity magazines)

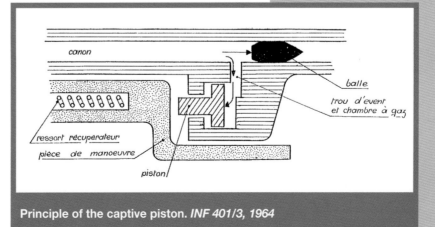

Principle of the captive piston. *INF 401/3, 1964*

Carry out safety maneuvers before any disassembly: open the bolt; visually check the absence of ammunition in the chamber. Let the bolt close; press the trigger while keeping the weapon pointed in a safe direction.

A. Unscrew the barrel band screw. You can use the base of a 30-caliber cartridge. You should not have to remove it completely; just loosen it nearly all the way.

B. Depress the band spring with a punch and use a nonmarring hammer to tap the barrel band down the barrel.

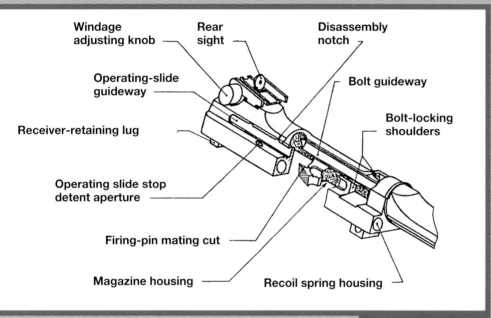

- Windage adjusting knob
- Rear sight
- Disassembly notch
- Operating-slide guideway
- Bolt guideway
- Receiver-retaining lug
- Bolt-locking shoulders
- Operating slide stop detent aperture
- Firing-pin mating cut
- Magazine housing
- Recoil spring housing

Receiver and bolt main parts. *INF 401/3, 1964*

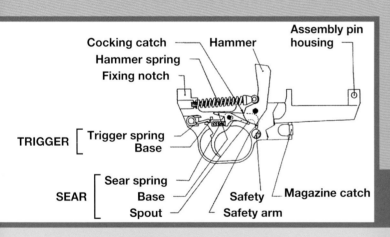

- Cocking catch
- Hammer
- Assembly pin housing
- Hammer spring
- Fixing notch
- TRIGGER
  - Trigger spring
  - Base
- SEAR
  - Sear spring
  - Base
  - Spout
- Safety
- Safety arm
- Magazine catch

Trigger housing. *INF 401/3, 1964*

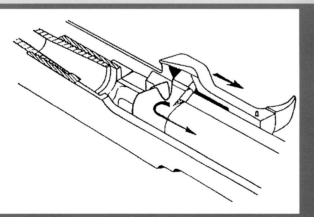

After a shot is fired, the gas operation drives the slide rearward, operating the bolt, which in turn ejects the shell casing in the chamber and strips a fresh round from the magazine while also cocking the weapon. A return spring manages the slide to its original position, ready to fire.

C. Remove the handguard up and out of the way.

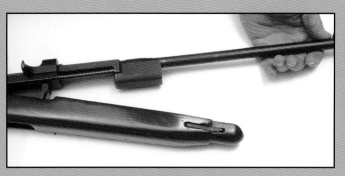

D. Remove the receiver and barrel from the stock by pulling up and then out.

E. Drift out the trigger-housing pin with a punch.

F. Remove the trigger housing from the receiver by pulling straight back and then pulling away

Disassembled carbine

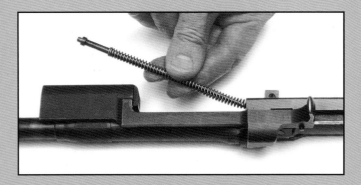

G. Pull back on the tip of the recoil spring guide, compressing the recoil spring, and move it away from the recess in the operating slide. Remove both the recoil spring and its guide.

I. Now push slowly forward on the operating slide while putting some counterclockwise rotational force on it. When the front of the operating slide reaches a notch on the underside left of the receiver, it will fall away. You may set aside the operating slide.

Two American combatants, one armed with a Thompson machine pistol and the other with an M1 carbine, on Corregidor in the Pacific

H. There is a notch along the receiver that allows the operating slide to be released. Pull back on the operating slide slowly while pulling it rightward. When it reaches the notch, it separates from the receiver.

J. Push the bolt back all the way forward and in the locked position. Now gently pull it rearward while putting counterclockwise rotational force on it. When the left front lug of the bolt reaches a gap in the receiver, it will disengage. You may now pull it up and forward to remove. If the rear snags, level the bolt by rotating back clockwise and continue to pull forward.

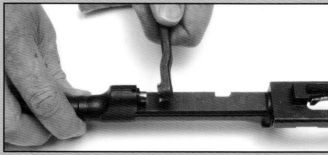

K. Pick up the barrel and locate the gas piston on the underside. Use the M1 carbine tool or a screwdriver punch to unscrew the gas piston nut. Doing this operation is not recommended even with a proper tool, because the gas piston is maintained in place by a needle punch and will need to be done again. Remove the gas piston.

OPPOSITE PAGE: Two variations of the M1 carbine and an M1A1 carbine with folding butt. The carbine at the top is mounted with a butt of early make, with the slot for the sling having a horizontal notch at each end, which leaves just a thin portion of the actuator (variation known as "high wood"). The carbine in the middle has a later wood; the sling slot has no notch at the ends, and the butt is machined in such a way that the actuator is more visible (known as "low wood"). The M1A1 carbine is mounted with the "low wood" type. There are also "high wood" versions of this butt. The three weapons are shown with accessories of the period related to the carbine: sealed metal box of 800 rounds, cardboard boxes of fifty cartridges, magazine pouches, and cleaning kit. US insignia and an M3 knife complete this picture.

CHAPTER 3

CONTRACTORS AND MANUFACTURERS

**It had been initially planned to hand over the production of the M1 carbine to two manufacturers: the Inland Manufacturing division of General Motors Corporation and Winchester Repeating Arms Company. The increase in demand during the war meant that other eight other companies were called on. Here, two carbines, one made by IBM and the other by Winchester.
*Marc de Fromont***

The American government initially entrusted the manufacture of M1 carbines to two firms:

- Winchester Repeating Arms Co.

- Inland Manufacturing Division of General Motors

When it became apparent that these two industrial companies alone would not be sufficient to satisfy the increasing demand for carbines, the Ministry of Defense studied the possibility of calling on other manufacturers and of multiplying the number of subcontractors to make secondary parts. To carry out this operation and to enforce the standardization of products and the total interchangeability of components, whatever their origin, the Carbine Industry Integration Committee was created, tasked with planning production of M1 carbines and their parts.

In addition to Inland and Winchester, who continued production of carbines, eight new manufacturers were selected. A further 1,500 subcontractors were called on to supply all ten manufacturers with the secondary parts necessary for the montage of the weapon.

In his study dedicated to the M1 carbine, author Bruce N. Canfield indicates that even among the ten makers of carbines, none had ever produced more than fifteen of the sixty parts that made up the weapon. The ten firms, traditionally listed as M1 manufacturers, are those whose identity is marked at the rear of the receiver on the weapon. These plants are those that carried out the final assembly of the weapons by using parts from various sources. The majority of them also produced receivers that bore their markings, but it will be seen in this article that there were occasionally exceptions to this rule. Some made barrels for their weapons, while others assembled

Aerial view of the
Winchester Repeating
Arms Co. in New
Haven, Connecticut

barrels on their receivers made by one of the other manufacturers or by one of the subcontractors such as Marlin or Buffalo Arms.

Here are the ten factories that made M1 carbines:

WINCHESTER REPEATING ARMS CO.

As has already been pointed out in the first part of this article, this famous firm based in New Haven, Connecticut, was at the forefront of the development of the M1 carbine. It was also the only one, out of all ten of the producers, to have solid experience in weapons manufacturing prior to starting manufacture of the M1 carbine. Winchester concluded a first contract on November 24, 1941, with the US government for the supply of M1 carbines, which was followed by seven others. In total it made 828,059 carbines (including 809,451 M1 carbines and 18,608 derivative models[1]) between September 1942 and August 1945. The Winchester marking on the receiver of numerous M1 carbines struck the imagination of their users far more than those of other brands, and it is not unusual to see the M1 carbine, even

in some French military manuals, designated as "Winchester carbine." If we consider the role this firm played in the development of the weapon, the use of the name was justifiable.

The receivers of these weapons bear the following markings above the serial number:

> TRADEMARK
> WINCHESTER

or:

> WINCHESTER
> TRADEMARK

Some carbines bear a house inspection stamp (the letters "P" and "W" interlaced in an oval proof logo at the rear of the receiver). Winchester in general made receivers and barrels identifiable by the letter "W" or by the initials "W.R.A."[2] struck on the upper surface, behind the foresight.

At the end of the war, the Ministry of Defense, predicting the approaching end of hostilities, canceled all contracts for the manufacture of M1 carbines, with the exception of those of Winchester and Inland. These firms bought out the stocks of the other manufacturers and used them for their own makes until August 1945.[3]

On the receivers made by Underwood (or supplied by the subcontractors to Underwood), taken over by Winchester, the letter "W" and "A" are struck at the rear of the receiver, sometimes separated by a stamp representing a grenade with a letter "W" in its center. The original manufacturers' markings are sometimes crossed out, depending on the manufacturer. The barrels of Winchester-

One of the variations in
the markings on the
receiver of Winchester-
made weapons. *Marc
de Fromont*

1. This expression designates the M2 carbine, a late version of the M1, fitted with a fire mode selector.
2. Unlike those of a lot of other manufacturers, it is common (but not systematic) that Winchester barrels are not dated. The barrels with a date and the initials "W.R.A." (Winchester Repeating Arms) are seen primarily on early productions.
3. In the last months of hostilities, the M1 carbines of the production lines in the Winchester factories (like those of Inland) were adapted to the manufacture of a version with selective fire: the M2, which will be studied later.

Two soldiers tasked
with radio operations
for the US 92nd
Division checking
telephone lines during
the German campaign
at the end of 1944.
US Army

View of the inside of the Inland factory: transport of weapons for testing. *Max C. Hayward*

Patriotic wartime poster in American factories

Marking on the receiver of an Inland-made carbine, which was the main producer of carbines during the Second World War. *Marc de Fromont*

The Inland factory in 1922 in Dayton, Ohio, with its logo inspired by the shape of the building

made carbines were marked "W.R.A." on the first makes, then simply "W." As on the other barrels, they bear the "flaming bomb" of the Ordnance Department surmounting the month and the year of manufacture (e.g., 3-44 for March 1944).

The buttstocks of these weapons are struck on the right side with the initials of the manufacturer, and also the initials of the military inspector who had supervised their reception at the Winchester factory:

> WRA
> GHD

There are two types of marking: with or without a frame. The letter "W" is also present on the left side, in the sling slit, and on the inside of the hand guard.

INLAND MANUFACTURING DIVISION OF GENERAL MOTORS

Based in Dayton, Ohio, on the site of the former workshop of the Wright brothers, pioneers of American aviation, Inland Manufacturing Division was a subsidiary of General Motors, developed in the 1920s to make steering wheels. This company subsequently varied its activities by producing very diverse consumer goods, from refrigerators to tractor parts. Even though these activities were initially quite far from the armaments sector, the

signs heralding the war had led this company to bring its support to the prototype of the carbine presented to the military tests by George Hyde. Despite the rejection of the Hyde prototype in favor of the one presented by Winchester, Inland was approached by the US Army to participate in the manufacture of the new M1 carbine.

Inland eventually became the largest producer of M1 carbines, making more than 2.6 million M1 carbines and derivative models[4] from June 1942 to August 1945.

4. Derivative models are the M1A1 carbines, a version with folding buttstock of the M1 and M2, which will be examined later.

Testing the M1 carbine in the Inland factory. *Max C. Hayward*

The receivers of these carbines have the following above the serial number:

INLAND DIV.

In addition, some receivers supplied to Inland by the Saginaw firm have the initials "SI" or "SG" on the left side of the receiver. These markings, generally struck fairly low on this part, could be seen only when the receiver was out of the buttstock.

The barrel bears this marking:

INLAND MFG. DIV
GENERAL MOTORS

The date of production of the weapon was stamped under the marking.

Some barrels, subcontracted to the firm "BLC" (itself a division of General Motors) for Inland, had, in addition to the marking mentioned above, the initials "BI" in front of the block housing the captive piston.

The buttstocks initially mounted on the Inland-made M1 carbines could carry quite varied markings: a grenade-shaped ordnance reception stamp ("flaming bomb") or crossed barrels on a belt and markings identifying the various suppliers that had made the wood for Inland: "O," "OI," "III," "SA," "LA," "Overton." The initials "O,"

On December 20, 1943, Gen. James Kirk received the one-millionth carbine out of the Inland factories.

Hartford, Bridgeport, and New Hartford, Connecticut. The first deliveries of carbines started in November 1942.

Underwood made great quantities of barrels for M1 carbines, and a part of this number was used by other makers (Saginaw, at its factory in Grand Rapids, Michigan; National Postal Meter; Standard Products Co.; Quality Hardware; and

The Underwood factory in Hartford, Connecticut

"OI," and "HI" are also found under the handguard on Inland carbines.

A lot of secondary parts, also produced by Overton for Inland, have the initials "IO" (Inland Overton) or the complete logo of the firm.

UNDERWOOD ELLIOTT FISHER

This famous typewriter manufacturer was the first to be identified by the American government (from March 1942 onward) to complete production of both firms previously named in the manufacture of M1 carbines. This firm adopted various measures to simplify the manufacture of certain parts as soon as it started production, in particular a trigger guard composed of soldered steel plates and a front sight obtained by stamping. The various components of the carbine were made in the principal factories of the Underwood firm in

Irvin-Pedersen) to assemble their own carbines. The exterior of Underwood-made barrels generally show visible traces of turning, to such an extent that this can be considered as a characteristic of this firm. The quality of the finish on the interior of the barrels is, on the other hand, excellent.

The receivers of Underwood carbines simply bear this marking:

UNDERWOOD

The presence of various initials is also noted frequently on these receivers ("B," "S," "W," "WA," "T," etc.), with the aim of identifying the factory that had supplied the original part. The rear of Underwood-made carbine receivers is sometimes also marked with a "flaming bomb" grenade, the symbol of the US Army Ordnance Department.

Marking of the manufacturer Underwood Elliott Fisher. A firm better known as a manufacturer of typewriters. The letter "B" appearing on the rear of the receiver identifies one of the 25,000 receivers supplied to Underwood by Singer. *Marc de Fromont*

The barrels have the same marking along with the date of manufacture of the weapon. By 1944, the US government started to predict the end of the war and began terminating contracts with many arms manufacturers, and, as a result, the surplus of unassembled parts from the Underwood factories were transferred to Inland. The original Underwood receivers used at the end of the war by Inland are marked as such:

-U-
INLAND DIVISION

The Underwood carbine buttstocks are marked with an inspector proof logo on the right side with the initials:

GHD
UEF

then:

UEF
GHD

Accompanied with an ordnance stamp (two crossed barrels on a circled belt).

It is extremely rare for an Underwood buttstock not to have an ordnance stamp. Whatever the seller may say, the absence of a proof logo on an Underwood buttstock indicates the use of a replacement part (it can also be the result of very enthusiastic scratching: we have seen the result!).[5]

The buttstock also carries initials stamped on the left side, at the entrance of the sling slit, identifying the various suppliers: "RMC," "M-U," "P-U," "LW," "LWY," "TN," "TRIMBLE."[6]

In total, 545,616 carbines were made by Underwood from November 1942 to April 1944.

Marking of a Rock-Ola-made carbine. This factory is also identifiable by the recoil plate tang on the buttstock. *Marc de Fromont*

ROCK-OLA

This firm, which originally made jukeboxes and slot machines, produced only 228,500 M1 carbines. Production started off arduously. Only 246 carbines were made in November and December 1942, and 10,005 during the first six months of 1943, due to the numerous difficulties concerning the organization of production. The government contract granting manufacture of carbines to Rock-Ola was terminated in May 1944.

5. This observation is also valid for the Rock-Ola and Saginaw carbines (except the buttstocks, which came from the canceled contract with Irwin Pedersen).
6. These precisions concerning the buttstock and handguard markings are taken from *The U.S. M1 Carbine* by Craig Riesch.

The Rock-Ola Manufacturing Corp. factory in Chicago

Equipment of an officer of the US 141st Infantry Regiment at the time of the Vosges mountain campaign. The M1 steel helmet is covered with a small-mesh net. The M-1941 cap is in olive green. The ensemble is the M-1943 jacket and trousers. When weather conditions were very cold, a thick lining (Pile Jacket Liner M-1943), made of poplin and an artificial fabric layer, can be worn, as seen here, under the jacket. The M-1936, on which were fixed an M-1923 pouch for two 45-caliber automatic-pistol magazines, a magazine pouch for the M1 carbine, and an M-1942 individual first-aid pouch, hang from M-1936 slings. The M1911A1 automatic pistol is held on the right in its fawn leather M-1916 holster. The M1 30.06-caliber carbine is a light weapon destined for officers and soldiers who did not need a normal rifle. The M3 knife is in its plastic M8 sheath. *Marc de Fromont*

On those carbines equipped with an adjustable rear sight, it covers partly, or sometimes completely, both the manufacturer's markings and the serial number, as on the M1 marked "Rock-Ola."

The receiver of Rock-Ola carbines is marked as such:

ROCK-OLA

It is also possible to encounter receivers supplied by Inland, on which the original maker's markings have been crossed through and replaced by "ROCK-OLA," usually stamped under the serial number.

The same marking is found on the barrel. In principle, only those barrels put into service before June 1943 are dated.

The buttstocks bear the ordnance logo representing two intertwined barrels and the initials "RMC" in a proof logo stamped on the right side. The initials RMC are also found on the left side in the sling slit and under the front stock.

Some parts of the mechanism, made by Rock-Ola (e.g., bolt head right lug, actuator, frame group, bolt tail portion), are marked "Rock-Ola."

Rock Ola supplied the wood to many other manufacturers of carbines.

QUALITY HARDWARE MACHINE CORPORATION

This company, based in Chicago, was dedicated before the war to the production of machine tools and stamped-metal components. From the beginning

Quality Hardware Machine Corporation business card

of the forties it began supplying the armaments industry with weapons parts (for .30- and .50-caliber machine guns as well as for Oerlikon antiaircraft cannon).

Quality Hardware Machine Corporation ("Quality HMC") was tasked with adapting the Spanish Star 9 mm Bergmann-Bayard ("9 Largo") machine pistol to .45-caliber American ammunition, subject to US Army tests.

After the project to adopt the Star was abandoned, Quality HMC was given an initial contract for the manufacture of 160,000 M1 carbines in March 1942. Several other contracts followed, and the number of carbines supplied to the American government by Quality HMC is estimated at 359,666 weapons.

"Quality HMC" marking

Infantryman of the US 1st Army at Werdau, Germany, in April 1945. *US Army*

The case of this firm illustrates perfectly the level of subcontracting reached in certain instances with the manufacture of M1 carbines. Between 1942[7] and 1944, Quality Hardware Machine Corporation mounted parts supplied by various subcontractors on its own receivers and also on receivers made by the Union Switch and Signals Company, a firm well known by collectors for having produced model 1911A1 pistols during the Second World War.

Toward the end of the war, Quality HMC engineers developed molding manufacturing processes for certain secondary parts (e.g., trigger guard). These techniques, designed to save both time and money, nonetheless arrived too late to be applied on a large scale for the manufacture of M1 carbines.

The receivers made by Quality Hardware Machine Corporation are marked as such:

QUALITY H.M.C.

The receivers supplied by Union Switch and Signals to Quality Hardware Machine Corporation are identifiable by this marking:

UN – QUALITY

The carbines made by Quality Hardware Machine Corporation are assembled with barrels supplied by various firms: Rock-Ola principally, but also by IBM, Winchester, Underwood, Inland, and Buffalo Arms.

7. In reality, the manufacture of carbines did not operate to full capacity before February 1943.

The buttstocks bear the initials identifying the manufacturer on the left side on the milling, where various slings pass. The majority of wood parts (buttstocks and handguards) used in the assembly of Quality HMC carbines was delivered by Rock-Ola and are marked "RMC" or "Q-RMC."

Business card of the National Postal Meter Corp. Inc.

NATIONAL POSTER METER

The manufacture of M1 carbines was initially entrusted to a subsidiary of this company called "Rochester Defense Corporation." It was, however, the name of the parent company that appeared on the receiver, marked as follows:

> NATIONAL
> POSTAL METER

National Postal Meter also used receivers supplied by Union Switch and Signal to assemble their carbines. These receivers bore the same marking as those made by National Postal Meter, but in addition they are stamped with a letter "U" under the serial number. Some receivers supplied by the Underwood or IBM factories are also used by National Postal Meter. In this case the markings of the original manufacturer are simply crossed through, and by a letter "N" stamped underneath, indicating its reuse by National Postal Meter.

At the end of the war, the firm was renamed "Commercial Controls Corporation." According to author Larry L. Ruth, after this change of company name, 239 unused receivers were marked

> COMMERCIAL
> CONTROLS

and were numbered from 0001 to 0239. These are among the rarest versions of the M1 carbine. National Postal Meter used only barrels made by other firms for these weapons, in particular Underwood, but also IBM, Marlin, Rock-Ola, or Buffalo Arms.

The buttstocks of these carbines generally bear the following marking:

> NPM
> FJA

In addition, some bear the marking "TN TRIMBLE" on the left side of the opening for the sling. The handguards are often marked "OI" or "TN."

STANDARD PRODUCTS COMPANY

Initially lined up as a prospective manufacturer of Springfield 1903 rifles by the Department of Defense, this producer of rolling stock was eventually entrusted with the production of M1 carbines. It made 247,160 of them, and the receivers bear this marking:

> STD. PRO.

Standard Products Co. never made barrels but mounted barrels made by Underwood, IBM, Inland, Marlin, and Buffalo Arms on its carbines.

Marking "National Postal Meter." The letter "U" stamped under the serial number indicates that this receiver was outsourced to Union Switch and Signals by National Postal Meter. *Marc de Fromont*

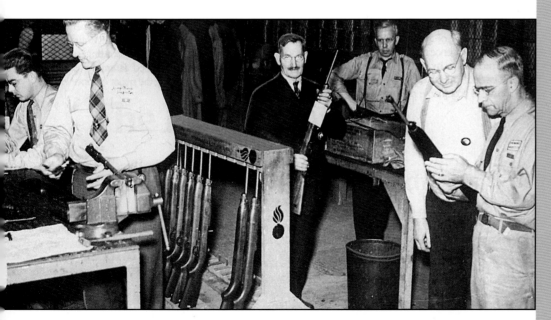

Final inspection of the carbines in the Standard Product factory. *Bruce Dow*

THE STANDARD PRODUCTS COMPANY
THERMO PLASTICS DIVISION

PLANTS
ST. CLAIR, MICHIGAN
PORT CLINTON, OHIO
CLEVELAND, OHIO
MARINE CITY, MICHIGAN

STEECHAN
TRADE MARK

PRODUCTS
MOLDED PLASTICS
STANDARD WINDOW CHANNEL
FOR AUTOMOBILES
MECHANICAL RUBBER GOODS
AUTOMOTIVE DOOR LOCKS
CHECKS & SUPPORTS

ADMINISTRATIVE & SALES OFFICE
505 BOULEVARD BLDG.
DETROIT, MICHIGAN

PLEASE ADDRESS YOUR REPLY TO
PORT CLINTON, OHIO

Business card of the Standard Products Company

Testing stand for carbines from the Standard Products Company

The buttstocks initially mounted on the carbines of this firm generally had the initials "SJ," and "S-HB." These markings are also found on the handguards.

IRWIN-PEDERSEN

This company was created as a result of the association between the Irwin brothers, industrialists in Grand Rapids, Michigan, and John Pedersen, a well-known weapons designer,[8] but was never able to establish carbine production from a technical perspective.

The US Army Ordnance Department canceled the production contract after the rupture of the receiver following the sixteenth shot during a firing test under the rain in the Aberdeen test center. Irwin-Pedersen had by then produced 3,542 carbines, none of which were accepted by the government.

The firm sold its equipment and spare parts in stock to the Saginaw firm, of Saginaw, Michigan, which also took over the old Irwin-Pedersen plant in Grand Rapids. After a period of reorganization, the production of M1 carbines was successfully relaunched.

Several thousand receivers made by Irwin-Pedersen were reused by Saginaw, but the figure 32,000 as quoted by Larry Ruth should be viewed cautiously since this marking is very rarely seen.

Irwin-Pedersen marking

Receiver of a carbine made by Saginaw Steering Gear Division of General Motors.
Marc de Fromont

Entrance of the Saginaw Steering Gear Division, Michigan

These weapons are seen with barrels of various origins: Underwood, Rock-Ola, Buffalo Arms, or Inland. The buttstocks can carry different stamps: RMC, RMC-FT, IR-IP, RSG, and O. The handguards are generally marked "IR-IP."

SAGINAW STEERING GEAR DIVISION OF GENERAL MOTORS

Here again we have another subsidiary of General Motors originally specialized in the manufacture of steering wheels, and other parts, for the automobile. As has been mentioned earlier, Saginaw produced M1 carbines in two separate plants: the main factory situated in Saginaw, Michigan (which authors often identify as "Saginaw Steering Gear"), and one in Grand Rapids, Michigan, which arose from the takeover of the former Irwin-Pedersen factory (this second factory is generally abbreviated to "Saginaw / Grand Rapids").

The receivers supplied by this Saginaw factory bear this marking:

> SAGINAW S.G.

The barrels mounted on these carbines have the marking "SAGINAW S.G."; the buttstocks can also carry the following markings: OI, RMC, TRIMBLE, TN, or RSG, on the left side in the opening where the sling passes. The right side has the letters "SG" and the usual ordnance logo. The handguards are generally marked RSG.

The receivers made by Saginaw in the Grand Rapids plant after the cessation of production of the Irwin-Pedersen firm are marked Underwood, IBM, Inland, Buffalo Arms, and Saginaw S.G

> SAGINAW S'.G'.

The carbines bearing this mark are seen with barrels of various origins:

8. To whom we owe the conception of the "Pedersen device," permitting the transformation of the Springfield rifle into a semiautomatic weapon, which was the unfortunate competitor of the Garand during the US Army tests of 1936.

The buttstocks and the handguards can either be devoid of markings or have the initials RSG, IR-IP.

Production of the main Saginaw plant and the Grand Rapids plant are estimated at 293,592 and 223,620, respectively.

INTERNATIONAL BUSINESS MACHINES CORPORATION (IBM)

This multinational firm, specialized in the production of calculating machines, which would become one of the giants of computing after the war, was, with Saginaw Steering Gear Division, one of the last two companies entrusted with a contract for the production of M1 carbines. The IBM company was however not a novice in the matter of armaments, since it had created a subsidiary to produce various military equipment in Poughkeepsie, New York, in 1941: the MMC (Munition Manufacturing Corporation).

The first contracts between the War Department and IBM were signed in early 1943 and were for the production of spare parts for M1 carbines. The first weapons were delivered in August of the same year, and the final twenty-five in May of the following year.

Among the many sites of this enterprise, the IBM factories of Rochester and Endicott produced diverse spare parts for the carbine, and the final assembly took place at Poughkeepsie.[9]

9. During the Second World War, the Poughkeepsie plant also made components for 20 mm guns and Browning Automatic Rifles (BAR). From 1942 on, the different IBM factories producing armaments were identified by a single number: the Poughkeepsie plant was designated under the name "factory IBM No. 4"; Endicott, "factory No. 1"; Washington, "No. 2"; Rochester, "No. 3"; and those of Toronto, Canada, "No. 5."

One of the carbine test sites after assembly in the IBM factory

Receivers made by IBM and others supplied by Auto-Ordnance[10] were used for these carbines. The IBM-made receivers are marked as such:

IBM CORP.

Those supplied to this firm by Auto-Ordnance also have the initials "A O" at the rear of the receiver. IBM made its own barrels for its weapons and also supplied other manufacturers, such as Quality Hardware Co., National Postal Meter, Standard Products, and Saginaw (Grand Rapids factory). The majority of IBM barrels made before 1943 are dated. The date of manufacture does not appear after this. The buttstocks on IBM carbines can have the following initials: B-RMC, BR-B, JL-B, LW-B, SC-B, and TN. The handguards are generally marked RMC, BR-B, JL-B, LW-B, or SC-B.

10. From 1940 to the end of 1942, Auto-Ordnance made Thompson machine guns in its own factory and also had them made by Savage. This contract for the manufacture of carbine receivers meant it could partially convert the activity of its Bridgeport plant.

PRODUCTION OF M1 CARBINES BY MANUFACTURER

Rock-Ola Music Corporation (ROCK-OLA)	228,500
Standard Products (STANDARD PRODUCTS)	247,160
International Business Machines (IBM)	346,500
Quality Hardware (QUALITY HARDWARE)	359,666
National Postal Meter (NATIONAL POSTAL METER)	413,017
Saginaw (SAGINAW DIVISION, GENERAL MOTORS) S.G.	293,592
Saginaw (Grand Rapids) S'G'	223,620
Underwood Elliott Fisher (UNDERWOOD)	545,616
Winchester (WINCHESTER)	828,059
Inland (INLAND DIVISION, GENERAL MOTORS)	2,642,097

This superb photo illustrates the large number of variations of American carbines, FROM TOP TO BOTTOM:

• **Rock-Ola Carbine**, barrel dated May 1943. The buttstock stamped "RMC" is an early-type sling slit in the shape of a capital "I"; wood is the Highwood type, leaving the actuator less visible; rear sight is in two positions; machined trigger guard; first-type barrel band; narrow tightening screws on the left side.

• **Inland Carbine**, barrel dated January 1944. The buttstock, stamped with the logo of the "Ordnance" (ordnance escutcheon), is of the second type, the sling slit is simplified, and the stock is cut in the same way as the handguard, clearing the totality of the actuator rod (low

wood). The other elements are comparable to the previous ones, apart from the actuator, which has an angular cut forward of the bolt lug ramp housing. This variation, named "60 o'clock M1" in the USA, was mounted only on Inland and Winchester carbines from 1944.

• **IBM carbine**, barrel nondated, made in January 1944. Same type of buttstock as the previous one. On this weapon the trigger receiver of the mechanism is not machined but is made in pressed steel. All IBM carbines are thus made, this variation being the only one produced by the IBM plant at Endicott. The breech is of the second type, round, but IBM also made flat breeches of the first type at the beginning of its production.

• **USM1 A1**, Inland made, barrel dated from June 1944. Apart from the "6 o'clock M1" actuator, this weapon is equipped with an adjustable rear sight (in pressed steel), a round breech, and a second-type barrel band (wider than the first, equipped with a housing for the barrel band spring head, tightening screws positioned at the lower part). The folding buttstock, of a "low wood" type, is one of the 300,000 extra frames produced after production of the M1A1 was stopped. This buttstock differs from original models on the following points: rivets on the leather cover are phosphate-coated (and not in darkened bronze) and the marking RI/3 is stamped on the grip.

• **USM1A1**, remounted by French army. This is a "Winchester" make with a nondated barrel, placed on an original M1A1 "low wood" buttstock. Barrel band main and top parts are of the first type. The leather cover was replaced, in the fifties, in a French army ordnance depot or a regimental workshop, and the three rivets used are of a very different model from the original.

These weapons are surrounded by accessories specific to this model: cleaning rod in two sections with metallic chamber brush and their transport pouch, magazine pouch for fifteen-round magazine, disassembly tools for the breech and the piston, M4 bayonet.

CHAPTER 4

MARKINGS

The marking "U.S. CARBINE CAL.30 M1" appears on the chamber of all M1 carbines. Depending on the manufacturer, the shape and the thickness of the letters could vary. Note that the Underwood receiver has the ordnance stamp at the rear.

An American soldier armed with this USM2 during the Korean War, in April 1951. *US Army Signal Corps*

Markings on M1 carbines enable today's collectors to determine if the parts of their weapons are original, and, if not, to find components that correspond to their weapon from the many spare parts still available.

On American carbines, only the receiver is numbered. The carbine parts supplied by the many subcontractors having taken part in their production program during the Second World War, as well as some spare parts made afterward, could be mounted on any M1 carbine with no fitting. The result of this total interchangeability was that the majority of carbines had one or several of the parts replaced, either through inadvertence when the weapon was reassembled after cleaning, or during repairs or reconditioning.

MARKINGS OF PRINCIPAL PARTS

A. Receiver

All receivers on M1 carbines made during the Second World War have this identification of the model on the chamber:

> U.S. CARBINE
> CAL.30 M1

The name of the company that was responsible for the final assembly of the carbine appears at the rear of the receiver, above the serial number of the weapon. This serial number was not originally reported on any other part.

It is possible to find ordnance stamps (grenade or barrels intertwined) on the receiver of certain carbines, but this was not systematic.

Some carbines, fitted with an adjustable rear sight and therefore with a serial number that was not very visible, had the serial number restamped in front of the rear sight.

B. Barrel

The name of the factory having supplied the barrel is generally mentioned on the top of the barrel at around an inch behind the foresight. It is important to note that the barrels can have a manufacturer's marking different from the one on the receivers.

Some Barrel Markings

FROM LEFT TO RIGHT:
"MARLIN" marking on a barrel made by this firm for some manufacturers tasked with the final assembly of M1 carbines.
Marking on a barrel made by Inland, a division of General Motors.

Marking on a barrel on an IBM-made carbine. These barrels stopped being dated from December 1943 onward.

Typical barrel markings: here, on an M1 carbine made by Underwood, the name of the manufacturer above the date, the ordnance grenade, and the "P" affirming that the barrel passed the tests. These markings were frequently simplified during the war.

During the Second World War, the US War Department entrusted the manufacture of barrels to a limited number of companies showing the required skills under the "Government Free Issue Barrel Program."

Among them some were also manufacturers of M1 carbines (such as Winchester, Inland, Underwood, Rock-Ola, Saginaw, and IBM). Others only supplied barrels and secondary parts (Buffalo Arms and Marlin).

This patriotic poster appeared in American production plants during the war.

Markings on two "Inland" made barrels dated May 1943 (5-43) and July 1942 (7-42). *Marc de Fromont*

The war in Indochina: a French parachutist armed with his USM1 alongside an injured soldier during Operation Castor in 1953. *Reportage Peraud-Camus*

Inspection proof logo stamped on carbine buttstocks from Underwood. The initials "GHD" are those of the military inspector attached to this factory; the initials "UEF" are those of the manufacturer: Underwood Elliott Fisher. "GHD" is the marking of Brig. Gen. Guy H. Drewry, an Army equipment inspector. There are also Underwood buttstocks that have only the Ordnance marking, but they are extremely rare and are found only on carbines dated 1944. *Marc de Fromont*

"NPM/FJA" inspection mark stamped on the buttstock of a carbine delivered by National Postal Meter. This is a final inspection stamp and not a simple manufacturer's marking. The first part is that of National Postal Meter, and the second is that of the military inspector (in this case, Col. Frank J. Atwood). The examination of these markings enables us to see if the buttstock corresponds correctly to the manufacturer of the carbine. Sadly, the effects of humidity and polishing on the wood have caused these precious indications, so appreciated by collectors, to disappear over the years.

M1 carbine made by Inland January 1945. The weapon has some end-of-production features: "low wood" and handguard with four rivets, adjustable rear sight in locally made stamped steel, a third type barrel band with bayonet holder.

M1A1 Inland carbine with barrel dated 6-44. This weapon is part of the second series of the M1A1, launched in May 1944. The remainder of the "high wood" from the first series was used without modifications until stocks were used up. Sometimes, as is the case here, it was assembled with second-type pistol grips, recognizable by the more prominent curve on the front. The presence of an adjustable rear sight (here a stamped model) and a wide barrel band is normal on a second-series M1A1.

The weapons are placed on a modified version of a USMC para camouflaged jacket worn by French Paras in Indochina. Also, a locally made bush hat, a USMC1 helmet with a French bandage placed in the elastic, a French Mle 1951 water bottle, and various documents: a booklet on Indochina and some Viet-minh tracts appealing to the French military to stop fighting. Also, insignia of the 1st Battalion Etranger Parachutist, the 1st Demi Brigade Coloniale of Commando Parachutist, the 3rd and the 6th Battalions Coloniale of Commando Parachutist, and the 8th Battalion Parachutist Colonial. *Marc de Fromont*

The date of manufacture of the barrel, in the form of a figure designating month and year, sometimes appears under the manufacturer's mark.

The "flaming bomb," which is the ordnance reception stamp, is often found under this marking. A letter "P" attesting that the barrel has been approved is found a little farther down (around 3 inches behind the foresight).

C. Buttstock and handguard

Carbine buttstocks generally have two types of stamps:

Ordnance inspection stamp on the buttstock of an M1 carbine. This stamp, appearing on so many American weapons parts, represents two intertwined barrels, a flaming grenade surrounded by a belt in the shape of a circle.

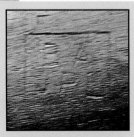

The initials "BA" are those of an arsenal that carried out the reconditioning of this carbine; the initials "JPL" are those of the military inspector responsible for receiving the weapon.

"RMC" inspection proof mark and a fine ordnance stamp on a carbine buttstock from the Rock-Ola factory

- Almost always present is a marking identifying the company that supplied the buttstock to the factory tasked with the final assembly of the weapon. These stamps can be found in different positions; however, they are most often found on the left side of the buttstock at the top part of the sling slit.

- Sometimes, although not systematically, military inspection stamps validating the compliance of the carbine before its departure from the factory: initials of the military inspector attached to the particular factory, accompanied by the insignia of the ordnance (showing two barrels intertwined on a belt in a circle, with the logo at the top; a minuscule flaming grenade; or, more rarely, a large, single flaming grenade). It is not unusual to see the logo alone on the buttstock, without the inspector's initials.

- Occasionally a letter "P" is found on the front or at the base of the pistol grip.

- Aside from original buttstocks, replacement ones can be found that were supplied during wartime (markings "IR," "PJ," "J," "LB," "LW"). In this case, the ordnance logo of the US Army is absent.

"PU" marking

"BR-B" marking

US Marine at Iwo Jima wearing an M41 jacket and carrying his USM1. *US Marine Corps*

Inland marking on a frame group

"IO" marking stamped on the inside of the stock of an Inland-made M1A1 carbine

• Carbine buttstocks having undergone reconditioning in the arsenal bear the initials of the arsenal or the factory that carried out the operation (e.g., "RIA" for Rock Island Arsenal, "AA" for Augusta Arsenal, "SA" for Springfield Arsenal, "U" for Underwood).

In addition, there is a stamp on the inside of the handguard, indicating the identity of the manufacturer.

After the war, some buttstocks continued to be made (from various woods) both in the United States and other countries that used this weapon; in particular, France, where the arsenals supplied replacement buttstocks for M1 and M1A1 to the army.

MARKINGS ON SECONDARY PARTS

Each carbine has a large number of parts made by outsourcing to factories of varying size. Sometimes these parts are devoid of any identification markings; however, most of the time they have one or two initials that identify the supplier. Dozens of letter combinations have been recorded, and several pages would be required to give a simple account!

Some larger parts are even marked with a logo visibly showing the name of the manufacturer; this is the case for example for certain Inland or Rock-Ola parts.

"W.U." marking on a hammer made by Universal Winding Co. for Underwood

A variation of the hammer marking "I-I"

LEFT: "Q" marking on a slide
RIGHT: "Y" marking and the component inventory number on another slide

Marking "JAO" and the component inventory number on an adjustable rear sight

Marking "JMO" on a barrel band

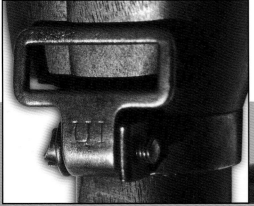

Marking "UI" on a first-type swing swivel

Marking "S," identifying the left side of a rear sight base

"M-U" handguard and magazine catch marking made by Marlin firearms for Underwood

"A-U" marking on a magazine catch. This marking remains unidentified.

"U" marking at the base of the trigger mechanism mounted on an Underwood carbine

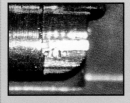

"U" marking on the locking stud on an Underwood bolt

Initials "EU" on the foresight support made by Prestole Div. Detroit Harvester

CHAPTER 5

VARIATIONS AND DEVELOPMENT OF M1 CARBINE COMPONENTS

WOOD (BUTTSTOCK AND HANDGUARD) AND MOUNTINGS

Varieties used

The majority of M1 carbines were originally assembled with a buttstock and handguard in walnut, and it was only during the final months of the war that beechwood was used. In his book *US M1 Carbines*, Craig Riesch points out that at the end of the war, the Rock-Ola company made buttstocks from cherry wood. In addition, due to the relative fragility of carbine buttstocks, it is not unusual to come across the so-called patched stocks, strengthened with metallic reinforcements.

Buttstock

On early-made buttstocks, the indentation where the sling passes has a profile of a capital "I" on the right side. This shape was swiftly abandoned in favor of a simple oblong cut. On early-made buttstocks, the actuator is partly hidden by the wood. This version is called "high wood."

From the very last months of the Second World War, the Fabrique Nationale d'Armes de Guerre in Herstal, Belgium, operated workshops tasked with repairing damaged weapons for the American army. This photo shows a repair workshop for M1 carbines. This category of weapon underwent many changes, which gives a high value to those that have kept their original state entirely. *FN*

Development of the weapon, FROM TOP TO BOTTOM:

• M1 made by Rock-Ola in 1943, with the oiler cutting an "I" and in "high wood"
• M1 made by Underwood at the beginning of 1944, in "low wood," with an oval cut for the oiler and trigger guard in pressed steel
• M2 reconditioned by Rock Island arsenal in 1952, during the Korean War. The weapon has an Inland receiver made in 1945, with a Springfield Armory barrel dated 6-52, and a molded foresight marked "R.I.A." The buttstock is a model called "Pot Belly," and there is the safety of the rotating model and magazine catch forward of the trigger guard. The magazine catch has the "M" marking indicating that it is the variety with three support points, designed to ensure an improved support for the thirty-round magazine (not shown in the photo). *Marc de Fromont*

Subsequently, the indentation made on the right side of the buttstock for the actuator was extended forward by about 8 cm. This larger cut made the actuator more visible. Buttstocks of this type are called "low wood."

At the end of the war, a buttstock with a slightly more bulbous-shaped stock[1] was adopted for the M2 carbine. Later, this type of buttstock was often mounted during repair operations on M1 carbines.

Handguard

Two main types of handguards were used during the Second World War for M1 carbines:

- On the first variety, the metallic grip plate on the inside rear of the handguard is fixed by two rivets (one on each side). There is a guideway at the top of the handguard, designed to free the sight line. This groove is very wide on early-made handguards (between 1.6 and 1.8 cm at the widest part). It was quickly noticed that a groove of this size reduced the weapon's resistance, and that a lot of the handguards split. The dimension of this notch was slightly reduced (1 to 1.5 cm) on the following makes.

1. Called "Pot Belly" by some authors

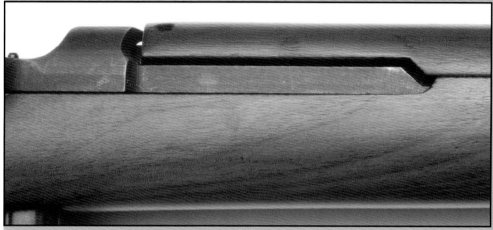

TOP: Early-made "high wood" buttstock, partly masking the forward extension of the actuator. **BELOW:** "Low wood" buttstock with an indentation frees the extension of the actuator.

TOP: Early-made buttstock with oiler housing in the shape of a capital "I"
BELOW: A later model with an oblong cut

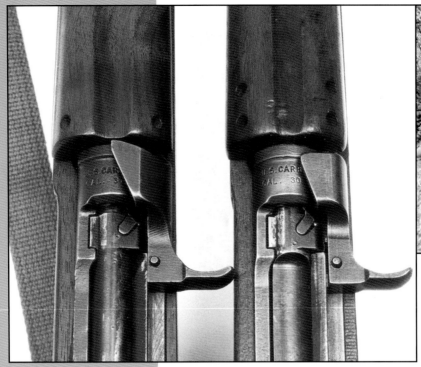

LEFT: Handguard with two rivets; **RIGHT:** handguard with four rivets appeared at the end of the war. This photo clearly shows the different shapes of the actuators.

The Indochina war: a snack break in the Tu Tan region at the end of 1952. In the foreground, an M1A1. *Indo-Editions*

FROM TOP TO BOTTOM:
Band of the second type (wide, with the screw positioned at the lower part)
First-type barrel band (narrow and closed by a screw placed on the left side)
Third type, similar to the previous one but extended by a bayonet)

- The second variant is distinguishable from the first by the presence of four rivets (two on each side), fixing the metallic grip plate positioned at the rear of the handguard. This variant, adopted in November 1943, was put into service from June 1944 onward at Winchester and Inland, the only firms making carbines after the month of May in that year.[2]

MOUNTINGS

Recoil plate tang

This part, screwed in the buttstock, at the rear of the receiver, had three variations (of which the two most common are shown below). Slight variations in the shape of the fixation screws and the screw bushing can also be encountered.

Butt plate

Depending on the manufacturer, the butt plates either had a square- or diamond-shaped grid pattern, with minor variations of patterns and borders according to the manufacturer and the time period.

Barrel band

Three main varieties of bands were used:

- The first is made of a narrow metallic strip closed by a screw on the left side, which holds a cut barrel band swivel in a piece of flattened metal. The hollowing in this part was initially fairly narrow and slowed down the movements of the sling. On later makes, this opening was enlarged to allow the sling to move more smoothly. During disassembly, this type of band remains solid with the barrel, and these parts can be separated only after the foresight has been positioned.

2. Handguards in perforated steel that are sometimes encountered are postwar.

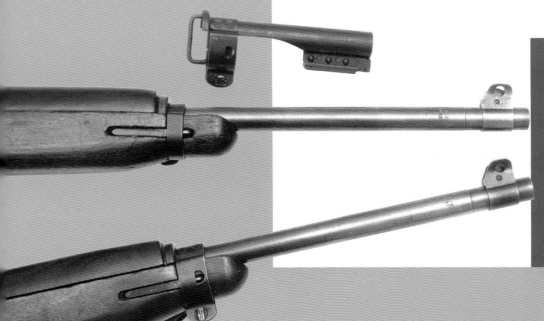

OPPOSITE PAGE: Reminder of the use of US M1 and M1A1 carbines in Indochina, the weapons shown here are surrounded by souvenirs from the French Expeditionary Force in the Far East: a "bob"-type bush hat, made from camo canvas from a US parachute, a machete, the insignia of the 8th Battalion Parachutist du Choc, a locally made leather holster for Colt 1911A1, and a cigarette case made after the war by the Viets with aluminum from planes shot down over Dien Bien Phu. *Marc de Fromont*

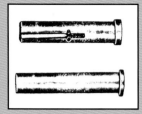

Frame group and receiver pin. TOP: old model with a maintenance spring; BELOW: new model. *US Army*

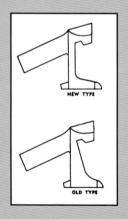

FROM TOP TO BOTTOM, two types of recoil spring housing: tube independent of the receiver (first type), and directly drilled in the surface of the receiver (second type)

Second-type barrel band

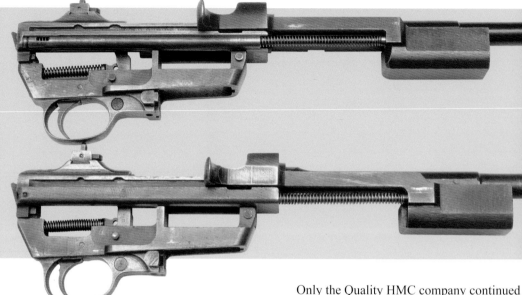

- The second, adopted at the beginning of 1944, is made up of a wider metallic strip, closed by a screw placed at the lower part. The sling ring positioned on the left side is usually made of folded steel wire.

- The third variation, adopted at the end of 1944, is identical to the previous one but is extended by a bayonet holder for an M4 bayonet.

A lot of carbines fitted with the first two types of barrel band were fitted with the third, bayonet type, during reconditioning.

RECEIVER AND ASSOCIATED ELEMENTS
Receiver
On the first carbines delivered by Winchester, Rock-Ola, and Quality HMC, the recoil spring was positioned to the right of the receiver in a tube but was independent of it (there are two variations of this tube). From mid-1943 on, Winchester and Rock-Ola adopted a new type of receiver with a reinforced base, already used by other makers of the M1 carbine. In this second type of receiver, the recoil spring housing is directly bored in the receiver block. This arrangement simplified the disassembly of the weapon at the same time as increasing the solidity of the receiver.

Only the Quality HMC company continued to deliver receivers fitted with an independent recoil spring housing until the end of its production.[3]

Receivers of the first type (fitted with an independent recoil spring housing) also show minor variations in the way the orifices for housing the actuator are arranged.

Rear sight
The first M1 carbines were delivered with a simple bracket with two positions (US Army Ordnance reference: B212605), for 150- and 300-yard distances. This rear sight was mounted in a machined dovetail above the rear part of the receiver.[4]

The carbine M1, having progressively come under the status of a close-quarter weapon, meant that its users did not delay in asking for a more elaborate rear sight.

3. This concerns only receivers made by Quality HMC and bearing this marking. Receivers supplied to this company by Union Switch & Signals (marked "U.N. QUALITY") are of the second type.

Receiver bases

Three types of rear sight, FROM LEFT TO RIGHT:
Rear sight with two positions
Adjustable rear sight, machined type, bearing the logo Helphill Mfg. Co.
Adjustable rear sight on a stamped model, marked "I.R.C.O." (for International Silver Co.). *Marc de Fromont*

A rear sight composed of an adjustable sight moving on a slanted ramp, calibrated from 100 to 300 yards and fitted with a windage adjustable knob, was adopted at the end of 1943. It was protected by lateral reinforcements mounted on the carbine in the same way as the version with brackets.

This second model of rear sight exists in two versions:

- the first, with machined lateral reinforcements (US Army Ordnance reference number: 6573955)

- the second, which is produced by a stamping process (US Army Ordnance reference number: 7160060)

These rear sights started to be fitted on carbines at the beginning of 1944, but the first model continued to be used, notably by National Postal Meter and Underwood. Normally a second-model rear sight would not be found on an original Irwin-Pedersen or Saginaw S'G' (Grand Rapids).

The reconditioning directives released after the war to the US Army repairs department[5] ordered the L-shaped rear sights that were initially mounted on M1 carbines to be replaced by adjustable rear sights. This fact explains the great number of carbines encountered today with the adjustable version.

Since the adjustable rear sight was much larger than the L-shaped version with a bracket, it was not unusual that the serial number of the weapon was concealed.

US Army equipment manuals foresaw this eventuality and ordered the weapon serial number to be stamped in front of the rear sight.

Frame group

Without going into too much detail concerning the minor modifications brought to the manufacture of the hammer, trigger, and trigger spring, we will endeavor to indicate the most-visible variations.

Trigger guard: the different types are

- machined or

- shaped from press cut steel plates and brazed side by side.

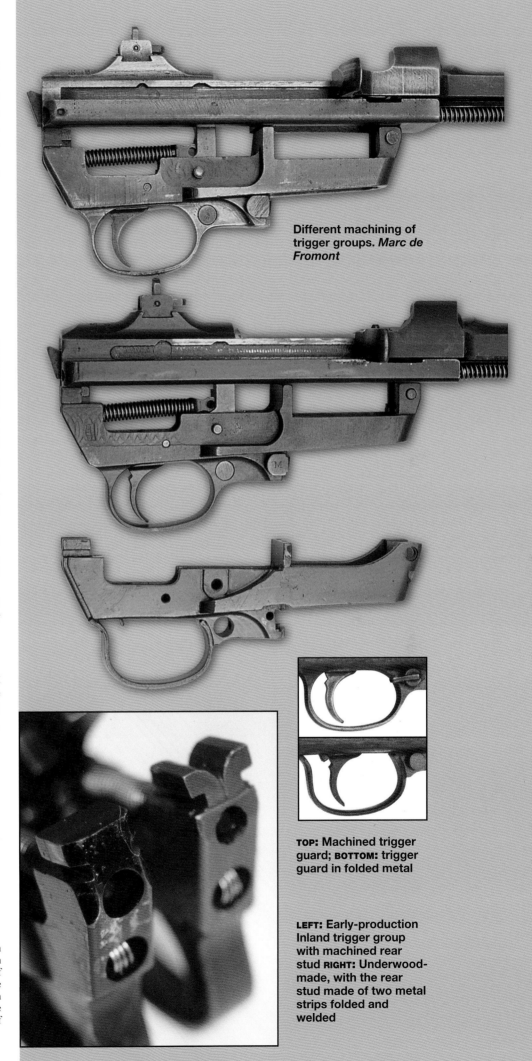

Different machining of trigger groups. *Marc de Fromont*

TOP: Machined trigger guard; **BOTTOM:** trigger guard in folded metal

LEFT: Early-production Inland trigger group with machined rear stud **RIGHT:** Underwood-made, with the rear stud made of two metal strips folded and welded

4. The support of these rear sights is generally stamped with a letter "S" on the left side. This letter prevents errors in assembly. The opening of the machined dovetail at the top of the receiver to receive the rear sight is in fact wider on the right side than the left. To mount an L-shaped rear sight with bracket on a carbine receiver, it must be introduced by the right so the letter "S" appears on the left side of the base of the rear sight.

5. Modification Work Order ORD B 28-W3

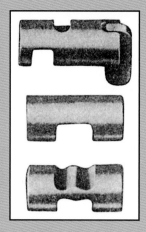

Development of safety levers.
US Army

Development of safety catches and magazine bolt levers, FROM TOP TO BOTTOM: safety catch and bolt lever are smooth; safety catch and bolt lever with grid pattern. Activated by a rotary-type safety and reinforced magazine bolt lever of the last type, conceived for the use of thirty-round magazines, as is indicated by the "M" marking on a line stamped on the other side of this part. *Marc de Fromont*

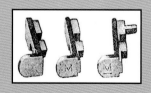

Development of magazine bolt levers.
US Army

Trigger and receiver pin

Initially this part was fitted with a thin spring designed to hold it solidly in place. Experience showed that the presence of a spring was superfluous and that its deterioration due to successive disassembly operations of the weapon could render reassembly difficult. A new pin devoid of a spring was therefore rapidly adopted (from early 1943 on), and the ordnance subsequently prescribed the systematic replacement of pins with a spring by single pins.

Safety

Both the magazine catch and the safety were initially activated by a catch. The safety catch had various surfaces: smooth, grid pattern, or with concentric circles.

A variation of the catch, with an internal machining slightly different from the one on the initial model, conceived to give a slightly gentler movement of the part, was adopted later.

However, complaints came from users because of errors resulting from confusion between the safety catch and the one on the magazine catch, with sometimes tragic results. This led to the safety catch being abandoned at the beginning of 1945 in favor of a pivoting lever with a guide, which was impossible to confuse with the magazine catch.

Magazine catch

American specialist authors count no fewer than a half-dozen variations in magazine catches. Without going into fine detail, some of them have a smooth lever, others are striated, and some have a letter "M." The latter is a reinforced model that American technical manuals recommended using systematically to replace old levers on M1 and M1A1 carbines when they passed through the armory.

The last version of this bolt, marked with a letter "M" on a bar, is marked with an extra extension on the left side, designed to support a third lug added due to the increase in weight of thirty-round magazines, which started to be produced for the M2 carbine from April 1945 onward.

Actuator

The specialist authors have identified six variations of this part, distinguishable by slight differences in the machining.

The cylindrical finger guard, placed near the bolt handle, was, to begin with, held in place by means of a pin, but this model was rapidly replaced by a simpler one, whose profile was to be modified again at the end of production.

M1 carbine from 1945 with two varieties of M4 bayonet and an M8A1 sheath

M1A1 carbine from the very beginning of the second series (May 1944). Although the weapon received the adjustable rear sight of the machined model and the wide barrel band, it is nonetheless fitted with a "high wood" stock completed with a first-type pistol grip. The rivets of the cheek rest are still in bronze;

Inland-made M1 carbine, barrel dated 1-44, equipped with "low wood." The three weapons have the last variation of slide, recognizable by the indentation at the front of the bolt handle. American collectors call this variety "6 o'clock M1" (there is also a "6 o'clock M2"). This type of slide is found only on Winchester and Inland makes. *Marc de Fromont*

Development of the shape of the actuator. *US Army*

M2

LEFT (CIRCLED): Slide stop catch on the first type of actuator. *US Army*

Moving bolt; IN THE FOREGROUND, with flattened upper surface (first type); IN THE BACKGROUND, with rounded upper surface (second type). This photo allows the different shapes of the actuator to be seen.

Soldier of the US 7th Army during the German campaign in the winter of 1944–45, wearing a reversible white/green parka and with a USM1 carbine in his muffled hands. *US Army*

Moving bolt

Two types of bolt were delivered:

- flattened in its upper part

- cylindrical body

In the first type there are two subtypes, with a wide extractor-housing notch and a smaller one. The first version was abandoned in favor of the second from the beginning of production, since ruptures in the right stud were observed during tests.

Slight variations were also introduced in the manufacture of various components of the moving bolt (extractor, firing pin, etc.)

It should be noted that although the majority of metallic parts of M1 carbines are phosphate-coated, the moving bolts in their original state are generally bronzed (many were, however, phosphate-coated later during the reconditioning process).

BARREL AND ASSOCIATED ELEMENTS

At the rear of the chamber, the barrels of M1 carbines were fitted with a wide circular reinforcement on slightly more than half their perimeter (from eleven o'clock to five o'clock if the rear surface of the barrel is compared to a clockface). This reinforcement was frequently damaged during production due to its length, so was reduced to a quarter of the circumference (from nine to twelve o'clock).

Gas block (or gas chamber)

Depending on the manufacturer, the gas block can be either machined in bulk or separately. Note also that there are at least two variations in the manufacture of the gas block piston and its bolt.

Front sight

The base of the foresight and the two lateral protective "ears," initially made by machining or stamping, started to be produced starting in May 1943 (from various times depending on the subcontractors supplying the parts) by welding or brazing of several parts made by stamping.

It is also possible to come across molded parts with the midpoint showing distinct run-out due to the unmolding process. The majority of collectors consider these molded units as replacement parts made after the war, but there is not absolute certainty concerning this. Some examples marked "R.I.A." (Rock Island Arsenal) have been observed on weapons reconditioned during the Korean War.

Yank magazine of the American army, dated June 1944, giving news from the front after the landings during the Battle of the Hedgerows

Reminder of the Algerian conflict with an M1 from 1945 and MA1 reconditioned by the French army, placed on a British army windproof jacket, modified by the addition of a zipper. **NEXT TO THE WEAPONS:** two French-made boxes of cartridges, a D37/46 grenade, and a "Bigeard" cap and an Algerian National Liberation Army badge taken as a trophy from a fellagha. Above the M1, badges of the 2nd REP (Regiment Etranger Parachutist) of the 1st RCP (Regiment du Chasseurs Parachutist) along with those of the 10th and 25th Parachute Divisions, alongside those of the Commando Force. The reconditioning of the M1A1 was the occasion to replace the original barrel band with a model fitted with a bayonet holder, on which an M4 bayonet is fixed. Remember that not one M1A1 carbine came out of a factory fitted with this accessory.

Rear reinforcement of the second-type barrel

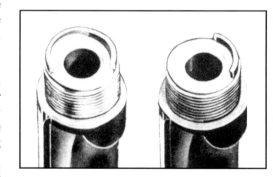

Both types of barrel reinforcements from a US Army official manual

Molded foresight, easily recognizable by the slight rough edge in the middle part

CHAPTER 6

DERIVATIVE MODELS OF THE M1 CARBINE

THE M1A1 CARBINE

Research was carried out on a version of the M1 with folding buttstock for airborne units.

After an evaluation of several models with buttstock folding under the weapon or laterally, a version fitted with a buttstock folding on the left side of the stock was adopted at the end of April 1942.

The manufacture was entrusted to Inland, which subcontracted the manufacture of the shorter stocks to the firm of S. E. Overton Co. of South Haven, Michigan, and the buttstocks to Royal Typewriter Co. of Hartford, Connecticut. The delivery of the first M1A1 began in November 1942.

During the Second World War, the carbines were widely used by American airborne units as well as by certain elements of the British Special Air Service (SAS). Some were also parachuted to resistance movements.

Patriotic poster displayed in American manufacturing plants during the war

Parachutist of the 502nd Parachute Infantry Regiment of the 101st Airborne Division armed with a M1A1 carbine in 1943.
US National Archive

They remained in service after the war in those armies with American equipment. The French army in particular used large quantities in both Indochina and Algeria. In 1981, it was still possible to see one of these M1A1 carbines as survival and self-defense equipment on board Puma air force helicopters.

The original M1A1 carbines are all made by Inland.

There were two distinct series:

• weapons of the initial series (around 71,000 produced from November 1942 to October 1943) showing features of the first type: "high wood," narrow barrel band, flat bolt, and "L" type of rear sight.

• Those of the second series (around 69,000 made from May to December 1944) are more varied and include successive modifications brought to the basic weapon, while also using the surplus buttstock elements produced for the first series still in stock. If the M1A1s of the second series are generally equipped with the adjustable rear sight, cylindrical bolt, and wide

A beautiful series of M1A1 carbines. FROM TOP TO BOTTOM:
French army reconditioning: bayonet holder and rivets in nickel-plated brass on the cheek rest
Second series with "high wood" stock but second-type grip and steel rivets on the cheek rest, adjustable rear sight in pressed metal
At the very beginning of the second series. Similar to the previous one, but with first-type pistol grip and bronze rivets on the cheek rest. The adjustable rear sight is the machined type.
"Hybrid" with a barrel dated 6-44, with its L-type rear sight and narrow barrel band, this weapon, with a second-series frame, is probably a reassembly.
Weapon of the first series with barrel dated 4-43 with "high wood" and first-type grip, bronze rivets on the cheek rest, L-type rear sight, and narrow barrel band. The rear of the stock has a "P" marking, which disappeared at the end of 1943. *Marc de Fromont*

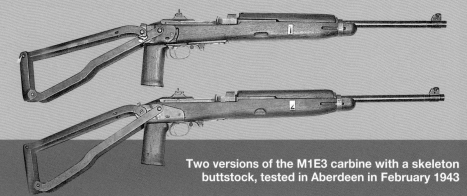

Two versions of the M1E3 carbine with a skeleton
buttstock, tested in Aberdeen in February 1943

The stock has a
housing fitted on its
left side for the cheek
rest of the metallic
buttstock when it is
folded.

Author Larry L. Ruth examining a prototype
of a US M1A1 at the Springfield Armory
Museum. *Collector Grade Publications*

RIGHT: US Army ordnance stamp at the base
of the M1A1 pistol grip. LEFT: "RI" marking
from the Rock Island arsenal at the base of
a replacement grip used for repairs

barrel band, they can be found mounted
on first-type buttstocks. What are
known as hybrid assemblies are also
encountered (wood of the first type
with a late folding buttstock with cheek
plate rivets in steel). Later makes have
an "end of production" type of wood:
a "low wood" buttstock, a handguard
with four rivets, a more curved pistol
grip, rivets in phosphate-coated steel
for the cheek plate.

On American-made war productions, the
rivets are in brass at the beginning of production
and later in phosphate- covered steel. Only the
material used is different; the shape of the rivets
remained the same.

After the war, some carbines were fitted with
an adjustable rear sight or a bayonet holder (or
both). Some mechanisms of various makes were
also able to be mounted at a later date on folding
buttstocks. In addition, many armies subsequently
made folding buttstocks on their own account;
currently it is not unusual to find buttstocks made
for the Dutch or French army, or more recently
for certain African armed forces. [1]

1. In particular buttstocks marked "FAZ" (Zaire Armed
Forces)

Commando-
parachutists with their
US M1A1 in the bush
during the Indochina
War. *Indo-Editions*

M1 and M1A1 carbines with "high wood"
The M1 is a Saginaw from September 1943,
the receiver of which is marked SG and not
S'G' or S.G.
The M1A1 is of course an Inland; the barrel
is dated 4-43. Note the bronze rivets on the
cheek rest and the shape of the pistol grip,
less curved on the first type than on the
second.
The weapons are shown with a US water
bottle and its cover, an M3 knife, and a US
M1C helmet with two boxes of fifty
cartridges inside, taken from their metal
container, which contained sixteen such
boxes. This collection is completed by a
badge from the 101st Airborne Division.
Marc de Fromont

On the buttstock of this M1A1 reconditioned by the French army, the leather-covered cheek plate has been replaced and fixed with the quite characteristic rivets in nickel-plated brass; the shape and diameter of the rivets vary depending on supplies available. The rivets are hollow. *Marc de Fromont*

Recruitment poster for US paratroopers. *US Army*

The butt plate bears the markings of the foundry.

First series with bronze rivets. These rivets have a very shallow concavity, and the edges are rounded.

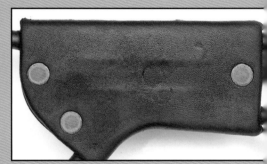

Reverse side of a first-series cheek rest with bronze rivets. Note that the rivets are flat and the metal is flush with the surface of the leather-covered cheek plate.

Second series with rivets in phosphate-coated steel; the manufacture and the layout are identical to the first series—only the metal is different.

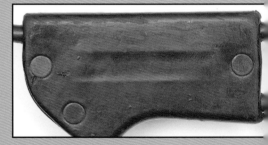

Reverse side of a second-series cheek rest with steel rivets

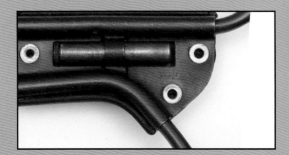

Buttstock reconditioned by the French army: leather replaced and rivets in nickel-plated brass

Version of the French army cheek rest. The left surface, with nickel-plated brass rivets, is curved and is therefore not flush with the surface of the leather-covered cheek plate.

THE M2 CARBINE

The development of a version of the M1 carbine with a selector on the left side of the receiver was initiated in May 1944. The selector allowed the user the choice between single-shot or continuous-burst fire.

The adoption of the M2 carbine went hand in hand with that of a thirty-round magazine. The thirty-round magazine was fitted with an additional lug and a device blocking the bolt in an open position at the end of the magazine, absent on the fifteen-round magazines used up to that point.

The first prototypes of this weapon were tested under the name "T4" in November 1944. Their mass production did not start before April 1945. Due to their late commissioning, these carbines were fitted from the start with a bayonet holder and an adjustable rear sight.

Only Inland and Winchester carried out the manufacture of M2 carbines. Production is estimated at around 500,000 examples for the first and 17,500 for the second. However, given the fact that kits permitting the transformation of an M1 carbine into an M2 were part of the equipment, it is possible to encounter M1 carbines of various makes transformed to the M2 version.

Original M2 carbines are marked thus:

> U.S. CARBINE
> CAL. 30 M2

At the critical time, Inland also produced standard receivers with the single marking "M," without the indication of the model. Depending on whether it was an M1 or an M2, they received the figure "1" or "2," struck by hand and more or less well aligned. These weapons are called "handstamped"[2] by American collectors.

This French soldier of the Korean battalion, with his thirty-round US M2, is equipped American style with walking boots and bulletproof vest. *René Bail*

Prototype of the M2 carbine made by Inland

M2 carbine with thirty-round magazine. This model is fitted with a beech "ventrue" buttstock (often called "Pot Belly" by American collectors), where the stock is much thicker than on initial models. *Marc de Fromont*

Marking on the chamber indicates an original M2 carbine.

FROM TOP TO BOTTOM: M2 carbine reconditioned during the Korean War at the Rock Island arsenal; the weapon here has a thirty-round magazine. M1A1 from the beginning of the second series, still fitted with parts coming from stocks of parts for buttstocks remaining from the previous series Carbine made by the Rock-Ola Manufacturing Co.; the barrel is dated 5-43 and has several features of the first types. *Marc de Fromont*

The "A" mark, for automatic fire, on a selector

At Winchester, the marking on receivers passed from "M1" to "M2"; the first M2s, still assembled from receivers marked "M1," received an additional figure "2" over the "1." American collectors designated these transition weapons "M2 overstamp."

After the war, other M1 carbines were reconditioned to M2 and the additional "2" on the figure "1" can be seen on weapons other than those of Inland and Winchester.

2. Marked by hand

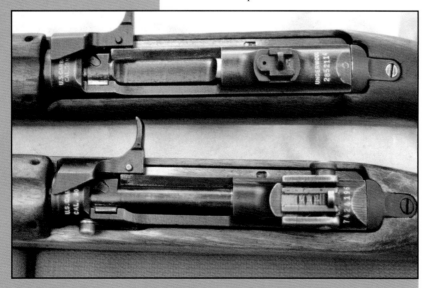

Comparison between an M2 receiver (BOTTOM) and an M1 receiver (TOP) Note the fire mode selector, on the left side of the receiver, and the adjustable rear sight on the M2 and the high serial number (greater than seven million) on this Inland-made weapon.

M2 carbine in action in Burma. *DR*

French soldier of the Korean battalion wearing the famous pile cap with ear flaps, holding his US M2 with thirty-round magazine. *René Bail*

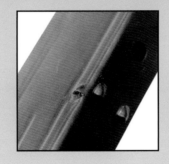

View of the magazine lugs. The lug added on thirty-round magazines to reinforce the weapon can clearly be seen on the left flank. The thirty-round magazine follower is designed in such a way as to serve as a bolt stop magazine follower, a feature that the users of the carbine complained of not having on a fifteen-round magazine.

Apart from this marking feature, and the presence of a mechanism permitting both single-shot and rapid-burst fire controlled by a selector placed on the left side of the receiver, the M2 had all the characteristics of late-production carbines:

- buttstock most often in beech, fitted with a reinforced stock (the "pot belly" shape) and the "low wood" used for the bolt handle

- round bolt

- adjustable rear sight

- barrel band ring with bayonet holder

- late-type swivel safety catch

- reinforced magazine catch designed to compensate the weight of the thirty-round magazine

M3 CARBINE

The last years of the war saw the development in both camps of night vision devices identifying the infrared light emitted by human bodies and objects giving off heat. This equipment was

relatively heavy and bulky, and in addition they had limited range. This led the American army to study the assembly of an infrared device on a carbine, whose moderate weight was offset by that of the night vision sight.

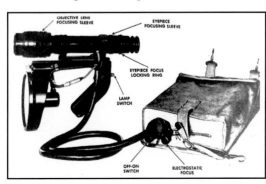

Firing an M3 with an "M2 Sniperscope." The knapsack is for the transport of batteries, with the connecting cable linking the batteries to the control grip positioned under the stock and the infrared projector under the telescope. The scope support was lengthened in relation to the T3 model. It rests on the barrel by a bracket that goes through a notch in the middle of the upper surface of the front stock. The infrared light projector was also sometimes mounted under the stock.

M2 sniper scope, connecting cable, and carrying case for the batteries

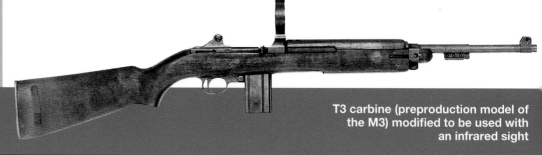

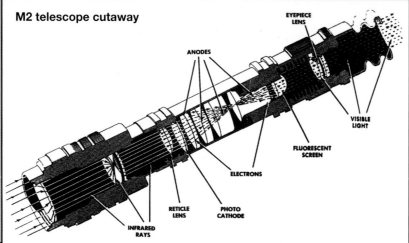

M2 telescope cutaway

ANODES
EYEPIECE LENS
VISIBLE LIGHT
FLUORESCENT SCREEN
ELECTRONS
RETICLE LENS
PHOTO CATHODE
INFRARED RAYS

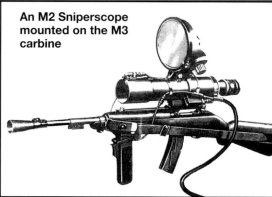

An M2 Sniperscope mounted on the M3 carbine

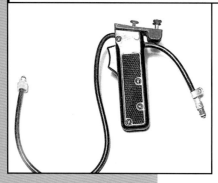

M2 grip

Use of the sight mounted on an M3 carbine for observation

Taking into account the performance of infrared equipment of the period, the limited range of the carbine was not really a penalizing factor.

At the beginning of 1944, a version of the M1 carbine with a receiver with bases allowing the assembly of an infrared sight device was tested. Only very small quantities of these weapons were made: 1,108 by Inland and 811 by Winchester.

The equipment of this weapon is composed of

- a battery carried by the operator in a knapsack and linked to the scope and a control grip by means of a connecting cable

- an infrared telescope

- infrared light projector positioned under the weapon and controlled by a trigger switch placed under the grip

Experience acquired with the T3 carbine gave rise to a series of this weapon designed to receive the M2 infrared sniper scope: the M3 model. Unlike the T3, which had the M1 carbine as a base, the base for the M3 was the M2. The exact name of this weapon is "Carbine, caliber .30 M3."

The M2 scope—the "infra-red M2 Sniperscope"—is mounted on a rail fixed at the rear, in front of the receiver, and extends as far as forward of the front stock.

The definitive version of this model was not adopted before August 16, 1945, just after the surrender of Japan. The M3 version would go on, however, to be used during the Korean War.

Infrared equipment, which allowed any heat-emanating body to be located in darkness, could be used as such:

- mounted on a weapon as a sight

- mounted independently to observe the terrain

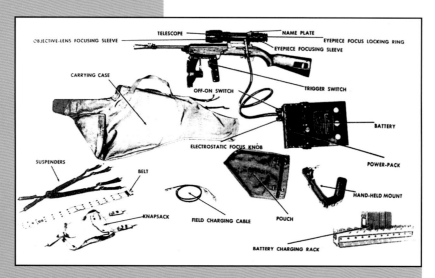

OBJECTIVE-LENS FOCUSING SLEEVE
TELESCOPE
NAME PLATE
EYEPIECE FOCUS LOCKING RING
EYEPIECE FOCUSING SLEEVE
CARRYING CASE
OFF-ON SWITCH
TRIGGER SWITCH
BATTERY
ELECTROSTATIC FOCUS KNOB
SUSPENDERS
POWER-PACK
BELT
HAND-HELD MOUNT
KNAPSACK
FIELD CHARGING CABLE
POUCH
BATTERY CHARGING RACK

Accessories relative to the M3 carbine and its telescope

CHAPTER 7

ACCESSORIES

M3 FLASH SUPPRESSOR

In night combat, the weapon's muzzle flash when fired reveals the position of the shooter to the enemy. When the M3 carbine, fitted with an infrared scope, was put into service, a conical flash suppressor with the same type of assembly as the M8 grenade launcher was also put into service.

M1 carbine fitted with its grenade launcher

The Pacific war: a group of Marines with their weapons. The M1 carbines are fitted with M8 grenade launchers. *US National Archive*

T.13 RECOIL CHECK

During the use of the M2 carbine, a recoil check meant to limit the upward movement of the weapon during rapid-burst fire was adopted. This accessory, with a seemingly limited effectiveness, had only a restricted use.

Technical notice for mounting the launcher for firing grenades on a permanently screwed mounting plate on the stock of the carbine

M8 GRENADE LAUNCHER

This accessory, adopted in March 1943, is composed of a simple tube that goes over the muzzle and is clamped onto the barrel on the front sight via a hinged door and wing nut.

This accessory is completed by an M15 grenade launcher sight, also used for Springfield 1903 and Garand M1 rifles. This launcher sight, carried in a canvas case that is hung on the belt, is fixed on a base permanently screwed on the left side of the stock.

CARRYING CASE

Various canvas carrying cases, generally with a zipper closing, were put into use to protect the carbines that were part of the weaponry on board vehicles. These cases were in khaki or olive drab canvas. Nylon cases were also used from the end of the sixties onward. Short cases,

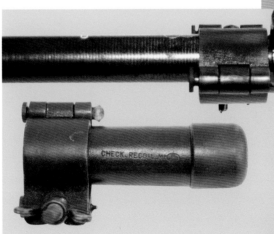

Recoil check: an accessory of controversial use that, in practice, was little used

sometimes fitted with belt hooks, meant the weapon could be carried at the belt in the style of a pistol. These were also put into service for the transport of the M1A1 carbine with folding buttstock during parachute jumps.

American soldier armed with his M2 carbine and its M3 flash suppressor

Carbine M1A1 in its parachutist case, with a Mk. II grenade, a maintenance manual, three variations of pouches for fifteen-round magazines (the one on the right is designed to transport two Garand clips instead of two carbine magazines), a 120-round cartridge belt on clips of ten, an M3 knife in its M6 case, a cleaning kit with its rod mounted, and badges of the 101st and 82nd Airborne Divisions. *Marc de Fromont*

Advertisement for Camel cigarettes in the January 1944 edition of *Life* magazine. The motorcyclists carry M1 carbines attached to their motorcycles.

French-made transport case for batches of maintenance equipment for M1, M2, and M3 carbines

In addition, leather holsters specially reinforced in order to avoid tears at the level of the bolt handle were put into service in certain mounted units and were particularly for the benefit of motorcycle units. This type of leather holster was also used for the transport of the weapon inside vehicles.

CLEANING KIT

This kit is identical to that used for rifles, but it has just two sections in the rod, one of which has an aluminum handle. The rod is transported in a canvas case (case cleaning rod M1), fitted with belt hooks.

This case has pouches containing a chamber brush in bronze wire, a pull-through, and sometimes a small brush.

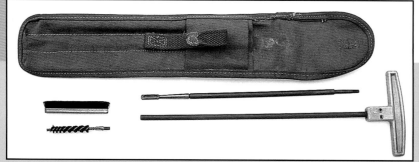

Content of a cleaning kit: a steel rod in two sections with aluminum handle, a chamber brush, a flannelette pull-through, and a small brush for cleaning the mechanism

Marking on the aluminum handle

Container of ten M2 carbines packed and attached head to tail, ready to be dropped. *Springfield Armory*

MUZZLE COVER

This is a sleeve in khaki canvas used to protect the muzzle and the foresight. A strap and a press stud keep this accessory in place around the barrel.

Tightness is adjusted by two press studs positioned on the strap, which means that this accessory can also be used to protect the barrel of the M1 and model 1903 rifle.

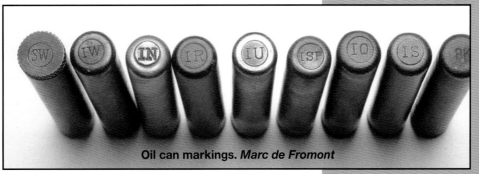

Oil can markings. *Marc de Fromont*

OIL CAN

This is a small cylindrical reservoir in phosphate-covered steel, which is used as a sling holder. This accessory was made by various subcontractors, the initials of which are generally marked on the extreme opposite of the muzzle cap.

BOLT DISASSEMBLY TOOL

This highly practical accessory is used to compress the extractor spring catch in order to disassemble the extractor. Once it is disassembled, the firing pin can be removed from the bolt with ease.

This tool is also used to facilitate the reassembly of the extractor.

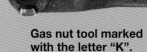

Gas nut tool marked with the letter "K". *Marc de Fromont*

Two Marines sheltering in a shell hole in June 1944 on Saipan island during the war against the Japanese. *US Army*

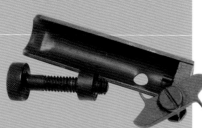

Bolt disassembly tool. *Marc de Fromont*

Arsenal Headspace field test bolt

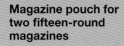

Magazine pouch for two fifteen-round magazines

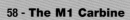

Manufacturer's marking and 1942 date, on the reverse side of a magazine pouch

TRIGGER SPRING DISASSEMBLY/ REASSEMBLY TOOL

This is a small, right-angled tube to compress the trigger spring to facilitate its disassembly, but principally its reassembly.

PISTON DISASSEMBLY TOOL

This tool is used to disassemble and reassemble the bolt holding the piston on the gas block. It is made from phosphate-coated steel and is generally marked with a letter "K." Its use remains exceptional for the reason pointed out in the chapter section "M1 Carbine Disassembly."

BLANK-FIRING DEVICE

Despite the fact that tests were carried out by the American army for the purpose of developing a device for blank firing, those that are generally encountered were produced after the war for the Dutch and West German (Bundeswehr) armies. These Dutch-made accessories were usually delivered with a bullet-casing deflector.

MAGAZINE POUCH

The American army used canvas pouches designed to transport two fifteen-round magazines.

Even though these magazine pouches were originally designed to be worn at the belt, they were soon used differently. When the mechanism is disassembled, it is easy to slide a pouch for two magazines around the buttstock. The weapon, with its magazine in place and two other magazines in the pouch placed under the buttstock, had, from that point on, an autonomy of fire of forty-five rounds (3 × 15), while remaining light, easy to handle, and balanced.

Blank-firing device for M1 carbine; this example made by the Dutch firm NWM for various NATO countries bears West German acceptance stamps.

A lot of soldiers used this option, and a number of USM1 buttstocks still today have the mark of the press stud placed at the rear of the magazine pouch, which immobilized it on the belt.

The French army modified the majority of original US magazine pouches that it used by riveting a fixation ring on the rear surface to the French leather suspension slings. The presence of this modification incited collectors to reject these magazine pouches. The popularity of material used by the French army during the campaigns of Indochina and Algeria means that these modified magazine pouches are now also much appreciated by collectors.

Magazine pouch modified by the French army by the addition of a ring on its rear side

AIRTRESS MIDLAND 1943

Metallic clip permitting two thirty-round magazines to be held head to tail. Note that one of the magazines is protected by a rubber cap.

At the end of the Second World War, magazine pouches to transport two thirty-round magazines and ammunition placed on clips started to make an appearance.

Outside of standard American-made magazine pouches, the wide distribution of the American carbine after the Second World War means that magazine pouches of all types and nationalities for magazines of fifteen and thirty rounds are encountered: German and Austrian, British, Israeli, Dutch, etc.

CLIP FOR TWO THIRTY-ROUND MAGAZINES

This is a clip in flexible steel designed to fix two thirty-round magazines head to tail, so as to carry them simultaneously on the weapon and to allow a rapid switching from one magazine to the other.

SLING

This is a strap in "web" material fitted with a metallic buckle at the rear and a stud and press stud at the front. It attaches to the left side of the weapon. The sling is fixed at the front of the sling swivels.

The rear part of the sling forms a loop that goes through the slit machined in the buttstock, where it is blocked by the oil can.

The early-made slings are made in light-khaki canvas; the olive-green version appeared at the end of the war. The fittings in darkened brass were later replaced by parts in phosphate-coated or black-painted steel. During the Vietnam War, nylon slings were put into service.

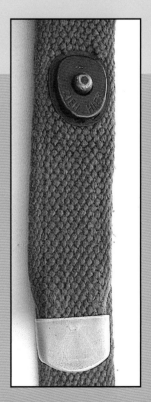

Dutch and German slings often had an aluminum tip.

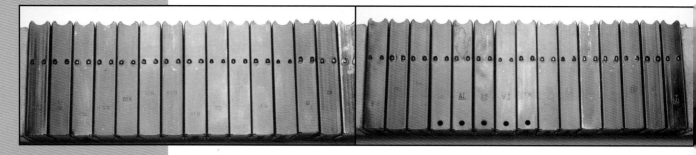

Variations in markings on magazines. *Marc de Fromont*

A Marine in Korea armed with his M3 carbine fitted with a flash suppressor and personalized with a wooden grip from a Thompson submachine gun. *US Marine Corps*

MAGAZINES

During tests that led to the M1 carbine being adopted, magazines of various capacities were trialed: fifteen, twenty, and thirty cartridges. Finally, a straight, fifteen-round magazine was initially adopted for this weapon. When the M2 carbine with selective fire was adopted at the end of the war, it was deemed necessary to use a magazine of greater capacity. A magazine of thirty cartridges with a slightly curved shape was subsequently put into service (there were two variations that have a different relief on the lateral surfaces).

These magazines were originally protected by a shiny black bronzing with a blue tint. They had a great variety of markings at the rear, which is a cause of great interest for collectors.

The magazines of five or six cartridges that are sometimes encountered were commercially made and were often put on the market after the war to conform with regulations restricting the holding of large-capacity magazines or their use for hunting. Many of these magazines were made from old fifteen- or thirty-round magazine stocks.

MAGAZINE DUST CAP

To prevent foreign bodies from entering the magazine, the American army put black or translucent rubber caps into service, which went on top of the magazine feed lips.

AMMUNITION BANDOLEER

This belt can carry six magazines of fifteen reserve cartridges or twelve clips of ten rounds wrapped two by two in cardboard.

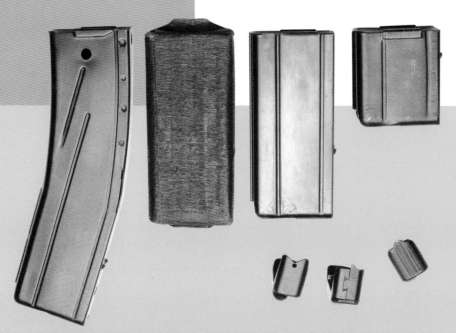

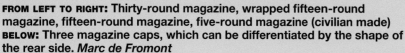

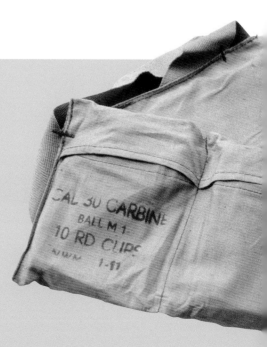

FROM LEFT TO RIGHT: Thirty-round magazine, wrapped fifteen-round magazine, fifteen-round magazine, five-round magazine (civilian made) **BELOW:** Three magazine caps, which can be differentiated by the shape of the rear side. *Marc de Fromont*

MANUALS

Numerous manuals on the US carbine were put into service initially by the American army but then by armies of many countries that used the weapon.

M1 carbine placed on a carrying case, with, **CLOCKWISE FROM TOP LEFT:** T23 flash hider; T13 recoil check; two varieties of muzzle cover; three varieties of fifteen-round magazine pouches (the one on the left is British made); maintenance manual (February 1943 edition); oil can with its original label; maintenance kit with assembled, two-section rod; disassembly tool for foresight (Dutch made for NATO); tool for disassembly of gas piston nut

Fifteen-round magazine, showing the frequent misuse of the dust cap designed to protect the top of the magazine and not the bottom; right-angled trigger spring disassembly and reassembly tool; M31 cleaning brush; bolt disassembly and reassembly tool; pouch containing an M15 grenade launcher sight and its accessories; early-type sling fitted with first-type narrow and inconvenient buckle; M4 bayonet in M8A1 sheath; metallic case of sixteen boxes of fifty cartridges, with one box placed next to it. This is a batch reconditioned in June 1944. The words "Steel Case" have been crossed out on the packaging, since they contain cartridges with brass casing. *Marc de Fromont*

Bandoleer for the transport of reserve clips

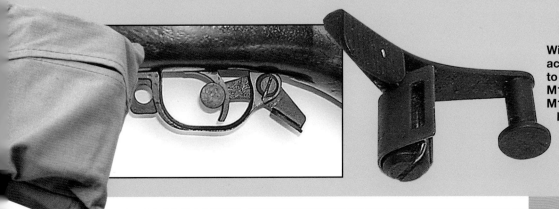

Winter trigger. This accessory is designed to be mounted on the M1 Garand rifle and the M1 carbine. For the latter it had an adapter that had to be screwed behind the trigger guard.

CHAPTER 8

THE M4 KNIFE BAYONET

Marines during the retaking of Seoul in the Pacific theater; the first with his M1 carbine, bayonet on the barrel. *US Army*

THE M4 BAYONET

When the M1 carbine was developed, no bayonet was included with it. However, it quickly became clear that the lack of bayonet was very badly received by troops armed with this magnificent small weapon. A report dated July 16, 1942, mentioned a bayonet tested on an experimental basis on the M1 carbine. However, because the head of the infantry and the head of the Bureau of Ordnance had decided, as a guiding concept, that there was no need to adapt a bayonet to the carbine, this test left no other trace, and it is possible that the bayonets made on this occasion were destroyed.

Before any other decision, the US Army Ordnance Department was asked to present its views

Winchester M1 rifle equipped with its M4 Camillus bayonet

concerning the use of a bayonet with the carbine, and what type to choose. A new project was initiated on October 28, 1943, to develop a model of bayonet adapted to the M1 carbine. This project allowed the development of several models of bayonets and adapters to mount them on the barrel of the carbine. Unfortunately, these bayonets appear to have left no trace in collections. It is, however, likely that their design was developed around the blade of the M3 knife, a shape of blade that would go on to be definitively adopted with the M4 bayonet and would have a great future becoming "the" model of blade for bayonets of NATO-affiliated countries, and even France would adopt it with its 1949/1956 first-type bayonet model.

On April 9, 1944, the new bayonet was adopted under the name "M4 knife-bayonet," at the same time as the new bayonet lug allowing it to be fixed to the carbine. On this occasion, and a mere fifteen months after its adoption, the M3 knife was decreed "limited standard," meaning it was no longer made and that its replacement was guaranteed only if stocks were available. Troops previously equipped with the carbine and M3 knife were scheduled to receive the M4 bayonet as a replacement of the knife, and this was then distributed to troops not equipped with the carbine. On May 10, 1944, the central equipment department sent construction tables to various contractors approached for manufacture, and production was started immediately.

The M4 bayonet is relatively short, very close to that of the M3, which took up its blade and handle. Only the cross-guard and the pommel changed. The total length is around 300 mm and can vary depending on the manufacturer.

M4 bayonets: TOP: Camillus-made, with plastic spacers near the cross-guard and pommel; **BOTTOM:** rare Utica-made bayonet with curved tip. This bayonet has an entirely leather grip.

French soldiers during the German campaign: here in street combat in Karlsruhe. *US Army*

The blade is 170 mm long, 22.2 mm wide, and 5 mm thick at the butt plate. Its general shape is symmetrical, with the point in the axis of the blade, and has a long leading edge with the counter edge on the opposite side about half the length of the blade. Toward the cross-guard, the sharp-edged tip is almost parallel and ends in a right angle, whereas the end of the counter edge is oblique and slightly concave. Some rare bayonets were made with blades from M3 knives and have this mark on the ricasso; they have the same manufacturer's mark on the cross-guard as on the blades.

This blade is extended by a rectangular tang on which the cross-guard, leather washers forming the grip, and a flat pommel were stacked, the whole secured by rivets at the end of the tang. The leather washers, around thirty, were shaped by turning them on a lathe after their positioning, in order to give the grip a thicker shape in the middle, becoming thinner toward the widening tip to seat both cross-guard and pommel. The rings near the cross-guard have flattened sides so as not to exceed the width. There are six grooves in the handle to allow for a better grip. These grooves vary in width from one bayonet to the other, depending on the manufacturer. Some contractors took the decision to position a fiber or plastic ring, the width of several leather rings,

at the end of the grip, in contact with the metallic parts. It was not, as has sometimes been written, a late modification, because only three manufacturers produced the bayonet with only fiber rings. This choice was probably taken to stop the cross-guard and the pommel from oxidizing too quickly, particularly in the tropical combat zones of Asia, since leather retained humidity much longer.

The cross-guard was stamped out of sheet metal, and traces of the process are visible on the sides. It has parallel sides, extended forward by a flat quillon with a rounded end. On the back the cross-guard widens from the muzzle ring, which has very thick side walls. The diameter of the muzzle ring is 14.9 mm. It is offset 8 mm from the back of the edge.

The pommel is made from an oval piece of solid steel, with a T-shaped slit at the back for the stud; this slit is open on the first leather washer. At the rear third of the pommel, on both sides of the slit, there are two grooves in which two hooks swivel, forming bolts, striated at their tips and held in locking position by two small spiral springs. The rivets forming the pivots of these bolts have a rounded head; their housing is most often extended by two small holes on the first leather washer. Some manufacturers rendered the fixation of these rivets with a hollow punch mark on the

Capt. Goupil, of the French battalion during the Korean War; he is wearing his bayonet in its sheath at the belt. *H. Segond collection*

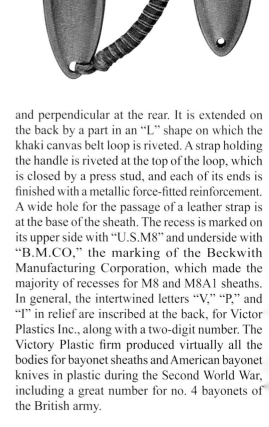

RIGHT, close-up of the orifices of the pommel rivets on two M4 bayonets; **NEAR RIGHT**, a Camillus with plastic spacers; **FAR RIGHT**, a Utica without plastic spacers

Two types of sheaths for M4 bayonets: **FAR RIGHT**, the M8 model without belt hook; **NEAR RIGHT**, the M8A1 model with belt hooks and leather lace

US Army Ordnance Department sheet dated May 13, 1944, showing specifications of the M4 bayonet and a list of contractors

rounded surface. The tang rivet is rectangular with slightly wavy sides and is struck with a "sun ray" mark typical of the M4 bayonet.

The metal parts of the bayonet are phosphate-coated with different tints, depending on the manufacturer. Sometimes the tang rivet is left in raw metal, meaning the part was assembled after the other constituent parts were colored. For this reason, the rear of the pommel can have a layer of protective black matte paint. In general, the blade is sharpened after the treatment of the metal, and in this case it has a glossy appearance and bears no trace of the original phosphate treatment.

The markings on this bayonet are in general those of the contractor on the front of the quillon, on the blade side, accompanied by the inscription "USM4" and the ordnance grenade. This type of marking is consistent on all M4 bayonets made for the US Army, but the ordnance grenade can also appear on the other side of the quillon. The pommel is generally stamped with the letters "I" and "S" intertwined. A number can also be struck on the pommel; it is possible that this corresponds to the type of treatment it received during manufacture. Some pommels are struck with an "H" in a shield in place of the "IS."

Even though it was possible to use the M6 sheath in leather from the M3 bayonet, it was decided to use only the M8 sheath for the M4 bayonet. This had a body in green laminated canvas, of a similar shape to the tip of the plastic sheath of the 1905 bayonet, with a flat surface ending in an oval on the top and the back and a flat flange around the entire perimeter. A sheet-metal recess is set at the top of the body by means of two small flaps folded in the lateral notches. The metal throat top plate conserved the extremities oblique due to the shape of the cross-guard on the M3 bayonet knife. This plate is point-welded on the recess by a flap turned down at the front

and perpendicular at the rear. It is extended on the back by a part in an "L" shape on which the khaki canvas belt loop is riveted. A strap holding the handle is riveted at the top of the loop, which is closed by a press stud, and each of its ends is finished with a metallic force-fitted reinforcement. A wide hole for the passage of a leather strap is at the base of the sheath. The recess is marked on its upper side with "U.S.M8" and underside with "B.M.CO," the marking of the Beckwith Manufacturing Corporation, which made the majority of recesses for M8 and M8A1 sheaths. In general, the intertwined letters "V," "P," and "I" in relief are inscribed at the back, for Victor Plastics Inc., along with a two-digit number. The Victory Plastic firm produced virtually all the bodies for bayonet sheaths and American bayonet knives in plastic during the Second World War, including a great number for no. 4 bayonets of the British army.

South Vietnamese Ranger armed with an M2 with M4 bayonet with leather handle in its sheath at his belt. *US Army*

Before the end of the war, the M8 sheath was replaced by the M8A1 sheath, from which it differed due to a longer belt loop so that it could be adapted to the standard double hook fastening to US belts. The recess is marked "U.S.M8A1" and "B.M.CO." The lace hole is still present, but during the war, it was never reinforced by a metal eyelet or even by a riveted metal tip. The sheaths equipped in that way were made after 1950.

The production of the M4 bayonet was on a large scale, since more than three million were made before the end of the war. There seems to have been no production after the war, but this point will be discussed later. Eight private firms received a contract from the Ordnance Department for the manufacture of this bayonet: Aerial Cutlery, marked with AERIAL on the cross-guard; American Cutlery, marked with A.C.C.; W. R. Case Cutlery, marked CASE; Camillus Cutlery, marked CAMILLUS; Imperial Cutlery, marked IMPERIAL; Kinfolks Inc., marked K.I.; Utica Cutlery, marked UTICA; and Pal Blade and Tool, marked PAL. The latter was also tasked with transforming 1905 bayonets into M1905 E1. By way of example, Camillus alone produced more than 301,000 M4 bayonets.

Aerial did not produce a lot of bayonets, and it is rare, even in the United States, to find a bayonet bearing the Aerial mark. The phosphate treatment of these bayonets is gray/green rather than black, and the riveting on the pommel is left white and sometimes painted in matte black. The bolt rivets are often marked with a punch mark.

American Cutlery was another rare producer of bayonets; the phosphate treatment is dark gray / green and the pommel rivets are left white.

Bayonets made by Case, even though produced in a large number, remain relatively rare. American collectors look for this make and command high prices in the United States. The particularity of Case bayonets is that the riveting on the pommel is convex, with no starburst stacking, is sometimes left blank, and is sometimes colored by a chemical process. The ordnance grenade struck on the quillon is transferred to the other, handle, side.

  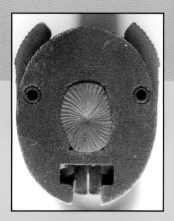 

Rear view of the pommel on an M4, made by Utica; note the "sun ray" and the roundheaded rivets.

M4 transition pommel from Camillus, marked "X"; the rivets have been punched for reinforcement.

Pommel of the M4 with plastic grip from Bren-Dan; in its best make, "sun-ray" and tubular rivets

M4 pommel made in Japan for the US firm Kiffe

The two M4s produced by Camillus: TOP, the most common model, with fiber washers on the handle; BOTTOM, the "transition" model. Note the deposits of the fungicide in the grooves at the junction of the cross-guard.

Camillus made two variations of M4 bayonets, one with fiber or plastic/laminated washers at either end of the handle, against the cross-guard and the pommel. The washer on the pommel side is indented for the rivets. The pommel is generally painted in black matte. The ordnance grenade is on the cross-guard side, turned toward the handle. The second variation of Camillus, much rarer, has no fiber washers, the leather being in contact with the metal parts. Its main feature is the cross-guard with a larger midsection; the edges of the quillon widen to become parallel with the middle of the cross-guard. The quillon is marked USM4 CAMILLUS, but the grenade is absent. The pommel is struck with an "X," and there is no indentation on the first leather washer. The leather is covered with a sort of adhesive varnish corresponding to an antimold treatment. It seems that this could be a "transition" bayonet distributed on a trial basis to troops in certain National Guard units in the northern and middle United States at the beginning of the 1950s.

The "X" struck on the pommel seems to confirm this hypothesis released by American historians. Examples encountered, generally speaking, are in good condition.

Two US soldiers alongside a field gun with the M4 bayonet at the belt. *US Army*

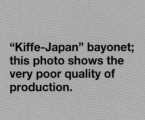

"Kiffe-Japan" bayonet; this photo shows the very poor quality of production.

At the end of the 1940s, a large number of M4 bayonets had to be reconditioned, the leather on the handles having deteriorated following poorly adapted storage. For this, at the beginning of the Korean War, the majority of bayonets in poor condition were sent to a state arsenal to be repaired. Some received new leather handles, but a considerable number of these bayonets were repaired by replacing the leather washers with a one-piece rubber grip in black. This new feature was exactly the same shape and size as the leather handle, with six grooves for a good grip. Since disassembly of the handle led to a slight reduction in the length of the tang, the rear part of the blade was ground down, with the result being that the cross-guard was nearer to the blade tip. This shortening of the blade, and so therefore the bayonet, is around one-sixteenth of an inch. The cross-guard is put back under force after this modification and held by the pressure of the rubber handle. There is a second type of one-piece rubber grip, extremely rare, which is generally associated with the Utica cross-guard marking: it is totally cylindrical, and the midpart has a slightly smaller diameter than the ends. This variation of handle also has the standard six grooves but they are closer together than on the other handle.

During the repair of these bayonets, the bolting system was also reviewed and the catch retainer pins were often changed. For this reason, those seen on these models of M4 bayonets have a different appearance, and it is even possible to find a roundheaded pin and one with a punch strike on the same bayonet. Sometimes traces from the grinding process are visible on the pommel. The finish of the bayonet was corrected, most often with black matte paint, and metallic parts were sometimes phosphate-coated again, and, in this case, the cutting edge was coated also. The tang rivet no longer has the "sun ray" design as on original makes but is made up of a certain number of round, adjoining marks. Certain cross-guards were replaced, and the new versions have a slightly different shape compared to the originals: the part between the quillon and the muzzle ring is slightly wider; the quillon keeps its parallel edges. These cross-guards are not marked and were probably made by the arsenal tasked with the reconditioning.

Imperial was the largest producer of M4 bayonets. There were no variations; all bayonets were of the same type, with fiber washers having contact with the metal. The leather of the handles can be subject to an antimold treatment, leaving a crystalline residue. Sometimes the pommels are marked with an "H" in the shield instead of the usual "IS."

Kinfolks produced bayonets with all-leather handles, with the riveting in blind stacking and a parkerized blue/gray finish.

Utica made two variations of the M4 bayonet. The first, and less common one, is recognizable by its cutting edge, which has a rounded tip instead of a standard right angle like the other manufacturers. The pommel is not marked and the riveting has blind-stacking and is left white, an often-unapparent feature since the pommel is painted in black matte. The second variation is similar to standard M4s, with the usual right angle. The riveting on the pommel is in a stacking arrangement, subject to bluing or blackened chemically but never painted. The pommel is marked with the standard "IS" with no number.

Pal made bayonets with resin washers, with contact with the cross-guard and pommel. The color of the phosphate coating was fairly light, and the catch retainer pins have rounded heads, but it is still possible to encounter those with a punched head.

The M1 carbine as the M1 Garand used in training in the US Army. *US Army*

The cross-guards are held in place by the plates and the sleeve's original forcing. These new plates are enveloping and the tang is not visible. Since the pommels were not dismantled, the bayonets kept their original length. The weapons were completely phosphate-coated during the repair, and this included the blades. It seems that only bayonets marked Case and PAL received this type of modification.

During the Korean War, the growing need for military equipment led to an increased need for M4 bayonets, and the US government decided to grant new contracts for the supply of this bayonet to private companies.

As far as the fixing of the cross-guard is concerned, it was decided not to weld it, so it could be changed easily if necessary. An 8 mm diameter hole was bored into the tang around 20 mm from the cross-guard, and a metal bar was inserted and bent into a "U" shape, thus forming a stirrup, toward the cross-guard, which secures it fully. The plates that were trialed were in aluminum, painted in brown or black. It is certain that these aluminum-plate bayonets were experimental, because the small number known in the US are not interchangeable but are adapted individually to each bayonet. Since the plates are thicker than the former leather grip, it was decided to widen the midpart of the cross-guard; therefore the edges of the quillon widen to become parallel with the midpart. It is the same type of cross-guard that is found on the Camillus "transition" bayonet. The new plates that were adopted are slightly shorter than the tang, which leaves a small space between the cross-guard and the plates, a feature that is also found on the M7 bayonet handles of the M16 rifle.

Another means of reconditioning M4 bayonets consisted of replacing the leather of the handles by a wooden one-piece grip of the same shape as the original handle, with two resin rings near the pommel and cross-guard. These new handles are not grooved but roughly file-cut with a very wide grid pattern, which certainly was done by hand since no two bayonets are exactly the same, nor indeed are the two sides of the handle on the same bayonet.

At the same period, several bayonets were repaired with black plastic plates with a grid pattern, fixed to the tang by two screws. To do this, the original tang was pierced with two holes.

During the Korean War, a group of stretcher bearers from a French battalion of the United Nations forces climb to the front. The man in the foreground has an M2 carbine.

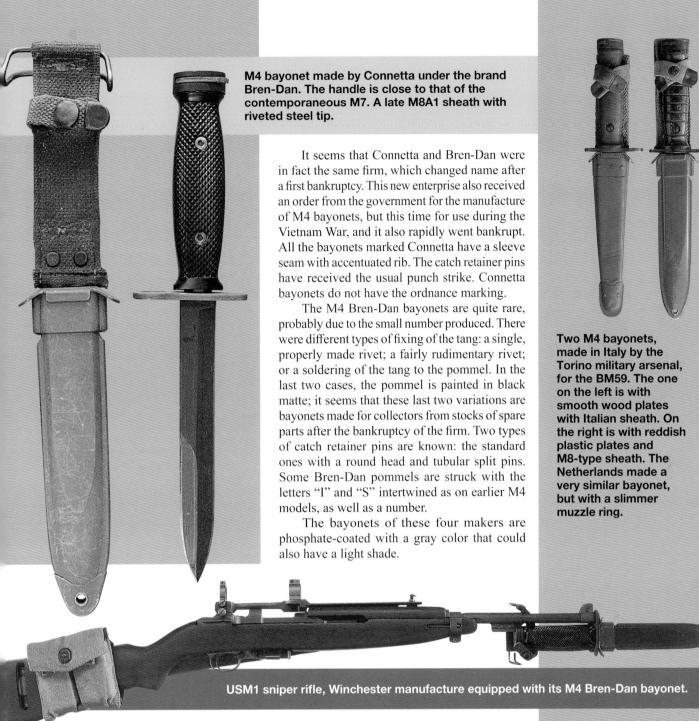

M4 bayonet made by Connetta under the brand Bren-Dan. The handle is close to that of the contemporaneous M7. A late M8A1 sheath with riveted steel tip.

It seems that Connetta and Bren-Dan were in fact the same firm, which changed name after a first bankruptcy. This new enterprise also received an order from the government for the manufacture of M4 bayonets, but this time for use during the Vietnam War, and it also rapidly went bankrupt. All the bayonets marked Connetta have a sleeve seam with accentuated rib. The catch retainer pins have received the usual punch strike. Connetta bayonets do not have the ordnance marking.

The M4 Bren-Dan bayonets are quite rare, probably due to the small number produced. There were different types of fixing of the tang: a single, properly made rivet; a fairly rudimentary rivet; or a soldering of the tang to the pommel. In the last two cases, the pommel is painted in black matte; it seems that these last two variations are bayonets made for collectors from stocks of spare parts after the bankruptcy of the firm. Two types of catch retainer pins are known: the standard ones with a round head and tubular split pins. Some Bren-Dan pommels are struck with the letters "I" and "S" intertwined as on earlier M4 models, as well as a number.

The bayonets of these four makers are phosphate-coated with a gray color that could also have a light shade.

Two M4 bayonets, made in Italy by the Torino military arsenal, for the BM59. The one on the left is with smooth wood plates with Italian sheath. On the right is with reddish plastic plates and M8-type sheath. The Netherlands made a very similar bayonet, but with a slimmer muzzle ring.

USM1 sniper rifle, Winchester manufacture equipped with its M4 Bren-Dan bayonet.

Four companies, of which three were new, received the government contract to make this new model: Imperial, with cross-guard mark IMPERIAL; the Turner Manufacturing Company in Statesville, North Carolina, with mark TMN; Connetta, with mark CONNETTA; and Bren-Dan, mark BREN-DAN.

The bayonets made by Imperial have the distinctive feature of having the pommel riveted at a very high temperature, which causes the tang and pommel to become almost welded together. The catch retainer pins have a punch strike. A new ordnance marking, an eagle head in a square, is struck at the rear of the cross-guard, near the handle.

The bayonets delivered by Turner have the standard tang rivets in "sun ray" and domed catch retainer pins. The pommel is often struck with a punch, similar to inspection marks seen on certain parts of US rifles of the time. The ordnance marking is not struck on the cross-guard.

A last type of M4 bayonet is also known; it was commercially made in Japan during the 1950s. Even though some claim that it was a contract granted by the US government to supply weapons to troops engaged in Korea, the majority of American collectors consider this model alone as a commercial bayonet. These bayonets have the mark "Rosco" in a diamond shape, and "Japan" on the flat of the blade, or the marking "Kiffe" and "Japan" on the blade, on the quillon or in the middle of the cross-guard. These bayonets can have various sheaths: the M8A1 model, a reused model, or one with a leather loop replacing the cloth one, principally with bayonets marked Rosco but also with the shorter M3 sheath with small, milled recess support hooks. The recess marking is original; "US" in the ordnance grenade or an "S" on its side was never struck on the M8 and M8A1, or even the USN Mk. 1 Navy sheath marking.

Bayonet dagger mounted on an American M1 carbine

Bayonet dagger, outside its scabbard, made after 1954 by the Henrion Conversat company in Nogent. In order to reduce the tendency of this dagger to break at the tip, a shorter and slightly thicker blade than the British Fairbairn-Sykes fighting knife was adopted for this French version.

The bayonet dagger in its scabbard. Unlike British knives, with a leather scabbard, the French version has a metal one suspended from a cotton cloth bayonet frog.

In 1995, the Camillus company made a commemorative model of the M4 bayonet taking up all the features of the original, except the leather of the handle is of a red color and they are in general delivered with the M6 leather sheath for the M3 knife. Some other commemorative bayonets were also made by Camillus during the 1980s, with very dark bronzed blades and golden engravings representing various battles in which the M4 bayonet had played a part.

The M4 bayonet was sold on as surplus by the United States to various countries, which could explain its relative rarity. Other countries took inspiration from this bayonet to create their own model, such as Germany, Italy, and the Netherlands, either for their own use or for the commercial market. The M1 carbine is still used in a number of countries, whereas the original bayonets, delivered with them, have now practically disappeared or been officially decommissioned.

BAYONET DAGGER FOR THE M1 CARBINE

This is a bayonet extrapolated from the dagger used by French marine commandos. This bayonet is specifically adapted to the M1 carbine. This weapon was principally used during the Algerian War.

This dagger takes up the general design of the British Fairbairn-Sykes fighting knife, although the blade is slightly shorter and less slender[1] so as to diminish the fragility of the tip, which represented one of the weak points of the British knife. It is equipped with a metal scabbard suspended from a cotton cloth bayonet frog. To use this bayonet, it was necessary to fix a particular bayonet support to the barrel of the carbine, on which the pommel of the dagger was locked.

A squad of marine commandos prepare their operation in Algeria. The officer in the center is pointing at the map with the tip of his bayonet dagger. *René Bail*

The bayonet differs from the standard commando dagger by its guard, with a ring on one side with an inside diameter corresponding to that of the US carbine barrel. It also differs by the presence of a cylindrical part on the pommel, with a groove that screws on to the rear part of the tang instead of the bolt slit usually mounted on standard-type daggers. This part, which is housed in an orifice corresponding to the adapter, is immobilized by two lateral screws that are housed in the groove.

Fixation of the pommel of the bayonet to the adapter

1. The blade measures 160 mm long, for a total dagger length of 274 mm. Depending on the versions, original British daggers can have a total length from 284 to 297 mm, with a blade length from 162 to 178 mm (figures published by Jean Fontvieille in his book *Couteaux de Combat*).

CHAPTER 9
AMMUNITION

In September 1940, the Ordnance Committee approved the project for the development of a new light weapon in .30 caliber. The announcement was made to manufacturers on October 1, 1940.

The first unnumbered drawing from WRA dates from October 2, 1940. The new rimmed cartridge came from the .32 WSL with rim.

Some modifications were brought to the initial design up until 1943. These were the following:

- on the bullet, with concave base then flat, or the presence of a groove for an improved crimping

- on the powder, IMR4227 then Hercules then Dupont EX4809

- on the tapering of the case; cartridges manufactured prior to June 11, 1943, sometimes chambered badly in later-made weapons

- on the noncorrosive priming, a condition indispensable to the longevity of the mechanism of the weapon and in particular that of the piston

The ammunition of the M1 carbine was almost called "Cal. .299 Ball M1" in order to avoid confusion with the new "Cal. .30, Ball, SR, M1" and the Garand cartridge ("Cal. .30, Ball, M1"), but it was not before September 14, 1944, that its official US name would be "Cartridge, Carbine, Cal. .30, Ball, M1."

The first known batches bore markings such as "WRA 30 SL" "REM-UMC 3SL," and "WESTERN 32 SL R," and it is possible there were test batches

without markings.
The marking of the very first lot would probably have had the letters "SR" for Short Rifle, but there are no known examples.

ORDINARY M1 BALL CARTRIDGES

These were produced by seven manufacturers:

- Frankford Arsenal: FA

- Western Cartridge Co.: WESTERN

- Winchester Repeating Arms Co.: WRA

A sergeant of the US II Corps taking a break in front of a First World War memorial during the Italian campaign

Diagram of the .30-caliber M1 cartridge

Ten-round clip

DATA	
Rim diameter	Dia. R: 9.01 (8.98/9.10)
Groove diameter	Dia. G: 7.70
Shell base diameter	Dia. H: 8.98 (8.95/8.99)
Neck diameter	Dia. M: 8.0 (8.40/8.45)
Bullet diameter	Dia. B: 7.79 (7.55/7.80)
Length of cartridge	LC: 32.70
Total length	LT: 42.45
Cartridge weight	WT: 12.20 g

VO: 464 m/s in a barrel of 127 mm equal to EO: 784 J for a projectile of 110 g

American ordinary bullet cartridges made during the Second World War, FROM LEFT TO RIGHT: WRA (44)—WCC 43 bullet in tombac-plated steel—RA 43—LC 43; the other examples on this photo are brass case, bullet with tombac jacket—LC 44—PC 44—EC 43 case in chromated steel.

OPPOSITE PAGE: M1 and M1A1 carbines about to go to the workshop. *Marc de Fromont*

- Remington Arms Co.: RA

- Kings Mills Ordnance Plant: PC

- Lake City Ordnance Plant: LC

- Evansville Chrysler Ordnance Plant: EC

In addition, various other types of cartridges were developed for the M1 carbine:

- tracer cartridge (red tip): M16

- high-pressure test cartridge: M18

- grenade cartridge: M6

- M13 dummy cartridge, of which there are at least two types

Box of fifty American-made cartridges

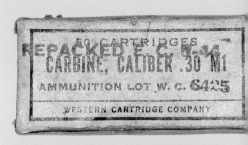

Box of fifty American made cartridges manufactured by Western Cartridge Company and repacked in 1944, as can be seen by the red stamp on the box

WRA 44 marking (Winchester Repeating Arms 1944). The star indicates that the cartridge was made at East Alton, and not at New Haven.

WRA 44 marking on a steel-cased cartridge

LC 4 marking on a brass-cased cartridge

EC 43 marking on a steel-cased cartridge with purple-coated primer

Two Dutch soldiers with American weapons in the 1950s; one with a Garand and the other with the M1. *Dutch Historical Service*

Several types of cartridges, FROM LEFT TO RIGHT:
Tracer bullet cartridge. M27 bullet with orange tip, LC 53.
Tracer bullet cartridge. M16 bullet with red tip, RA 44.
Tracer bullet cartridge. M16 bullet with red tip, PC 43.
Tracer bullet cartridge. Blue tip bullet, LC 52.
Cartridge Viper (Remington R.P.) .30 caliber tinned-brass case
Test cartridge M18 WRA 52 tinned-brass case
M7 grenade auxiliary cartridge for launching grenades

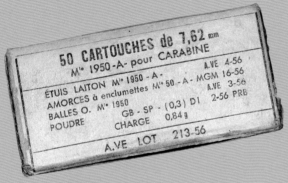

French box of fifty cartridges, 1950 model, made in 1956 A.VE (Valence Workshop). French carbines for M1 carbine could have the Berdan or Boxer primer, in which case the year 1950 was followed by the letter "A."

TRACER CARTRIDGES

The development of the M16 tracer (with red tip) was carried out at Remington beginning in August 1943 at the request of the British forces in Burma. The production took place at Remington and at Lake City.

Other tests were carried out on the M16 at Frankford Arsenal.

The M27 tracer bullet (orange tip) was conceived so it lit up only at around a 50-meter distance from the barrel, making the shooter's position less easy to identify.

TEST CARTRIDGES

The M18 and M18 (modified) were made by Winchester and Frankford Arsenal. They have an ordinary brass case and a .30 M2 with or without grooves. Great care must be taken with the various fakes. It is very important to refrain from firing this type of cartridge in an M1 carbine (pressure reaches 50,000 psi) due to the risk of overpressure.

PROPULSIVE CARTRIDGES

In February 1942, Frankford Arsenal developed a blank cartridge to launch the M9A1 antitank rifle grenade to 200 yards at the speed of 144 fps. M6 with FA, WCC, LC, and EC markings can be found.

The range of rifle grenades can be increased by placing (rim forward) the M7 cartridge on the mouth of the grenade launcher tube before covering it with the grenade; it is fired by the shooting of an M6 propulsive cartridge. The M7 cartridge was nicknamed the "Vitamin Pill" by American troops.

It was C. R. Olsen, at Frankford Arsenal, who developed the auxiliary cartridge to improve the range of rifle grenades. This device was in the shape of a large, short cartridge with red rim and cap, nonprimed.

Blank and propulsive cartridges, FROM LEFT TO RIGHT:
West German blank: DAG no marking, Ringdal patent
Norwegian blank: Bakelittfabricken SA, no marking, Ringdal patent
Norwegian blank: Bakelittfabricken SA, no marking, Ringdal patent
Dutch NWM .30 57, Belgian FN, American LC53 propulsive M6
French GEVELOT (7.62)

Marking of a KTW cartridge with bullet covered in Teflon

French military marking SF 4 I 50

R-P 30 carbine marking

Training cartridge on a scale of 1 to 2 next to a commercial Norma cartridge with semiarmored bullet

Dummy cartridges, FROM LEFT TO RIGHT: American, WRA 44 M13 first type; German, Geco 30 M1; French SF I 4 50 factory dummy; American, LC 43; French, VE N 4.60 7.62; French, VE S 2.60 7.62; American, WRA 44 M13 second type; French VE N 4-60 7.62.

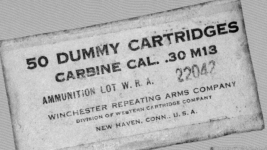

Box of fifty dummy cartridges for the M1 carbine made by Winchester Repeating Arms Company (WRA)

Box of thirty-six French cartridges made at the Valence cartridge factory in 1949

DUMMY CARTRIDGES

The first type of dummy cartridge of June 1942 had a tinned-brass shell and was nonprimed. The second type, from March 1944, had a brass case pierced with two holes: the housing of the primer is empty, and the vent holes can either be pierced or not; subsequently it was the jacket of the projectile that would be tinned.

Apart from these standard ammunitions, there were many rare varieties resulting from the numerous studies led both during and after the Second World War. But there is little chance that today's collector would encounter authentic examples of ammunition such as a US blank cartridge of the Second World War, a "fragile" with a green-and-white tip, an armor-piercing type with black tip, or a lead hunting cartridge destined to be part of the survival kit of shot-down aviators or for spotting ammunition with a silver tip.

Various cartridges, FROM LEFT TO RIGHT: American with Teflon-covered bullet, KTW (Kopsch, Turcus, and Ward); French ordinary bullet, TE C 4 55; R-P .30 carbine test cartridge; Dutch ordinary bullet NWM 54; Dominican, 30 M R 59 D; Swedish commercial with semiarmored bullet, NORMA US .30

CHAPTER 10

A CONTROVERSIAL WEAPON

During the war in the Pacific, two Marines armed with their M1 carbines equipped with M8 grenade launchers. *US Marine Corps*

T he M1 carbine was certainly one of the most popular, but also one of the most controversial, weapons of its time.

The majority of users come under the spell of this small carbine due to its lightness, accuracy, firing procedure, balance, elegance, and ease of maintenance.

However, even today its efficiency during combat is often called into question. The stories of enemy soldiers continuing to advance—and even to fight—when they had been hit several times by the carbine are numerous. But apart from the fact that these are often secondhand stories rather than firsthand witness accounts, it still raises the question that if an adversary had received the same number of projectiles in the same circumstances from another individual weapon, would there have been a different result?

The "miracle projectile" that stunned or stopped any adversary in his tracks is just a myth; it is the injuries inflicted by a projectile that count: the most powerful projectile of a war rifle, even fired at a short distance, will not guarantee the immediate neutralization of the adversary unless it hits a vital organ.

It is certain that the projectile of the M1 carbine would rapidly lose its power and its stability at medium distance. But the weapon and

Marines on Iwo Jima fighting the Japanese, March 1945. *US Department of Defense*

its ammunition had been designed for close-quarter combat. A lot of postwar French military manuals clearly point out that the effective range of this weapon is 200 meters.

Two main elements harmed the reputation of the excellent small M1 carbine:

- Its appearance: it is a shoulder weapon, with the receiver and the bolt strongly reminiscent of the M1 Garand rifle, and this meant that the M1 carbine was often considered as an undersized version of it. In this light, any comparison in terms of range, long-distance accuracy, and firepower prove unfavorable to the carbine. Considering the initial mission of this weapon and the features of its ammunition, it would be more reasonable to make comparisons between its performance and those of pistols and machine pistols in service.

- The drift concerning tactical use: initially conceived for men whose main purpose was not fighting with a rifle, it was rapidly distributed in a large number to frontline combatants. The carbine was called on to fulfill a

mission for which it had not been designed. From then on, it would be illogical to criticize the weapon and its ammunition for its limited range.

These elements could have led to it being shelved, but the fact that this weapon, of which more than six million remained in service for almost fifty years, is remembered with favor by the vast majority of its users highly commends it.

The .30 M1 cartridge was also used

- for handguns, such as certain Smith & Wessons rechambered in this caliber by Israel in the first years of the Jewish state, some versions of Ruger Blackhawk and Contender and Kimball, and AMT "Automag III" semiautomatic pistols

- for hunting carbines, such as the Marlin 62 model

- for assault rifles and semiautomatic carbines, and the Cristobal carbine with the mechanism derived from the Beretta machine pistol, but also a series of French assault rifles and semiautomatic carbines studied in French arsenals during the 1960s

M1 carbine placed on a camouflaged jacket next to a Colt 1911A1 and a regulation US machete. Note the sealed metal box of ammunition on the right of the photo.
Marc de Fromont

Young female guerrilla fighter in Salvador, 1982. *UPI*

During the Second World War, an ever-increasing number of Allied combatants were equipped with the M1 carbine or the M1A1 with folding buttstock.

The armistices of 1945 (with Germany and Japan) led to the manufacture of the M1, M1A1, M2, and M3 carbines being stopped, but did not signal its withdrawal—in fact, quite the opposite:

- In the United States, the carbine continued to be used intensively by the armed forces during the Korean War and at the beginning of the conflict in Vietnam. Many carbines stocked in the US were destroyed or delivered in the name of military aid, so their manufacture was subsequently relaunched by a number of private enterprises such as Plainfield, Iver-Johnson, or Universal to be used by police forces or sports marksmen.

- In the French army, the M1 carbine was widely used during operations in Indochina and Algeria. In the eighties, M1 and M1A1 carbines were still used as a protection-and-survival weapon by certain helicopter crews of the ALAT and the Air Force.

- In the rest of Europe, the majority of NATO armies used M1 carbines. The Dutch army in particular used it extensively during guerrilla operations in the West Indies. The various German police forces, the border guards (Bundesgrenzschutz), and the first units of the West German army (Bundeswehr), during its reconstruction, were widely equipped with American carbines.[1]

1. Tens of thousands of M1 carbines were repaired and reconditioned in Belgium by the Fabrique Nationale d'armes de Guerre de Herstal. In Germany, the Erma company made some spare parts to ensure the carbines used by the German army police could be maintained.

M1 carbine modified for the German police. The original rear sight has been replaced by a sighting notch positioned above the chamber. Note that this carbine made by Inland has a very low serial number (17741). The last four figures of the serial number are also on the slide. *Marc de Fromont*

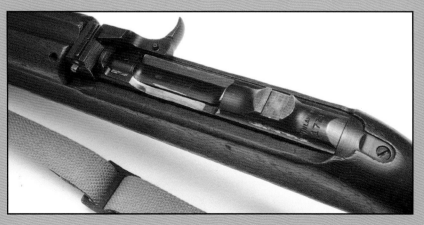

Bundeswehr mountain troops armed with the M1 carbine. *Bundesminister für Verteidigung*

Throughout the world, the M1 carbines and the diverse versions of them remain widely used still today: in particular in Asia and Latin America, where both their lightness and small size are highly practical for the nature of the terrain and the morphology of the inhabitants of these regions.

Gen. Douglas MacArthur said the carbine M1 was "one of the strongest contributing factors in our victory in the Pacific." We conclude this special edition by stating that the M1 carbine was an overall success and more than fulfilled the mission that it was initially given.

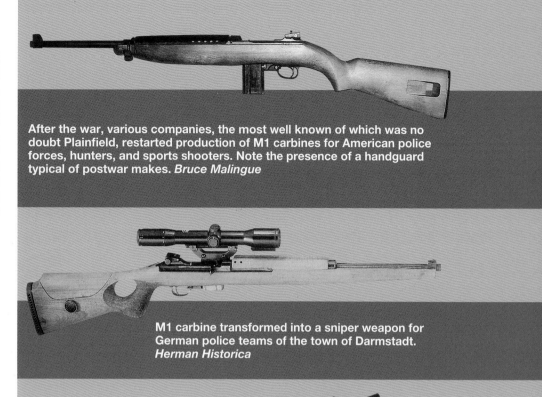

After the war, various companies, the most well known of which was no doubt Plainfield, restarted production of M1 carbines for American police forces, hunters, and sports shooters. Note the presence of a handguard typical of postwar makes. *Bruce Malingue*

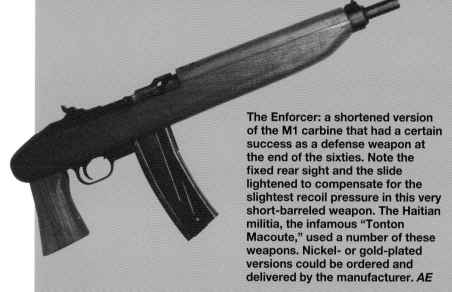

M1 carbine transformed into a sniper weapon for German police teams of the town of Darmstadt. *Herman Historica*

The Enforcer: a shortened version of the M1 carbine that had a certain success as a defense weapon at the end of the sixties. Note the fixed rear sight and the slide lightened to compensate for the slightest recoil pressure in this very short-barreled weapon. The Haitian militia, the infamous "Tonton Macoute," used a number of these weapons. Nickel- or gold-plated versions could be ordered and delivered by the manufacturer. *AE*

French infantrymen in the Mulhouse region during the Battle of Alsace at the end of November 1944

BIBLIOGRAPHY

THE WEAPON

Canfield, Bruce N. *Bruce Canfield's Complete Guide to the M1 Garand and the M1 Carbine*. 2nd ed. Lincoln, RI: Andrew Mowbray, 2010.

Hufnagl, Wolfdieter. *US-Karabiner .30 M1: Waffe und Zubehör*. Stuttgart: Motorbuch-Verlag, 1994.

Huon, Jean. *La carabine U.S. M1*. 3rd ed. Chaumont, France: Ed. Crépin-Leblond, 2004.

"M1 Carbine Owner's Manual M1, M2, and M3 .30 Caliber Carbines" (republication of the regulation manual "TM 9-1276, TO 39 A-5 AD-2," of the US Army, 1953).

Riesch, Craig. *The U.S. M1 Carbine: Wartime Production*. 4th ed. Tustin, CA: North Cape, 2002.

Ruth, Larry L. *M1 Carbine: Design, Development & Production,*.Highland Park, NJ: Gun Room, 1983.

Ruth, Larry L. *War Baby! The U.S. Caliber .30 Carbine*. Edited by R. Blake Stevens. Toronto: Collector Grade, 1992.

Ruth, Larry L. *War Baby! Comes Home: The U.S. Caliber .30 Carbine*. Vol. II. Edited by R. Blake Stevens. Toronto: Collector Grade, 1993.

Schreier, Konrad F., Jr. *The M-1 Carbine*. Los Angeles: Petersen, 1973.

AMMUNITION

Ermeier, Hans A., and Jakob H. Brandt. *Manual of Pistol and Revolver Cartridges*. Vol. II. Schwäbisch Hall, Germany: Schwend, 1980.

Hackley, F. W., W. H. Woodin, and E. L. Scranton. *History of Modern U.S. Military Small Arms Ammunition*. Highland Park, NJ: Gun Room, 1978.

Huon, Jean. *Les cartouches pour fusils et mitrailleuses*. 2nd ed. Chaumont, France: Ed. Crépin-Leblond, 2006.

Jorion, Serge, and Philippe Regenstreif. *Culots de munitions: Atlas*. 2 vols. Toulouse, France: Cépaduès, 1994–95.

Regenstreif, Philippe. *Tout savoir sur les cartouches: Identification par leurs marquages colorés*. Versailles, France: Sofarme, 1981.

Various articles appearing over the years in specialist magazines: *La Gazette des Armes*, *Action-Armes et Tir*, *Cibles*, *AMI*, and others.

CLASSIC GUNS OF THE WORLD SERIES